The Marian Dimension in the Apocalypse of St. John

Frits Albers Ph.B.

Edited by
Frank Calneggia

En Route Books and Media, LLC
Saint Louis, MO

ENROUTE
Make the time

En Route Books and Media, LLC
5705 Rhodes Avenue
St. Louis, MO 63109

Cover credit: Sebastian Mahfood

ISBN-13: 979-8-88870-521-6
Library of Congress Control Number:
Available online at https://catalog.loc.gov

Dedication

To my wife Barbara

and

the lively Decade God has entrusted to our care

Anna, Rosemary,

Nicholas,

Genevieve, Elizabeth, Jacinta,

John-Paul,

Yvonne, Monica,

Michael,

this book is gratefully entrusted

Table of Contents

List of Old Testament Abbreviations Used in the Text

Am	Amos	Ba	Baruch	1 Ch	1 Chronicles		
Dn	Daniel	Dt	Deuteronomy	2 Ch	2 Chronicles		
Ex	Exodus	Ezk	Ezekiel	1 K	1 Kings		
Gn	Genesis	Hab	Habakkuk	2 K	2 Kings		
Hg	Haggai	Ho	Hosea	1 M	1 Maccabees		
Is	Isaiah	Jb	Job	2 M	2 Maccabees		
Jg	Judges	Jl	Joel	1 S	1 Samuel		
Jon	Jonah	Jos	Joshua	2 S	2 Samuel		
Jr	Jeremiah	Lm	Lamentations	Lv	Leviticus		
Mi	Micah	Ml	Malachi	Na	Nahum		
Nb	Numbers	Ne	Nehemiah	Ob	Obadiah		
Pr	Proverbs	Ps	Psalms	Qo	Ecclesiastes		
Rv	Revelation	Ws	Wisdom	Si	Ecclesiasticus (Sirach)		
Tb	Tobit	Sg	Song of Songs				
Zc	Zechariah (Zacharias)	Zp	Zepaniah (Sophonias)				

As a rule, the References used in this book have been taken from the *Jerusalem Bible*, the Standard Edition, 1966.

The number in square brackets, [ ], refers the reader to the page in this edition of the *Jerusalem Bible* where the quote can be found. This is done to facilitate looking up the context from which the quotes have been taken.

The number in ordinary brackets, (v.), indicates the verse in the Chapter of the Apocalypse presently under discussion.

As the Reader will discover, the Number of each SECTION of the book corresponds with the CHAPTER of the Apocalypse being discussed in that SECTION. The LIST of Old Testament References after each Section refers to the identical Chapter in the Apocalypse. This List is by no means exhaustive, but helps to bring the Reader in contact with the incredible riches the Old holds in store for the understanding of the New. In this I have followed the safe guide of the work of Fr. H.B. KRAMER, and the research undertaken by the compilers of the *Jerusalem Bible.*

Fr. Kramer's outstanding work *The Book of Destiny* was the Commentary, and the constant companion at my side for the basis of my own work. I thank God that it has been written, even if it is in need of extension in one dimension. This extension is hereby provided.

Foreword

The is a book about Hope

In a time

- in which Abortion is unrestricted,
- in which Euthanasia is round the corner,
- in which children are given the right to sue their parents for not having been aborted,
- or for having been educated in the Christian Religion;

in a time when it becomes almost impossible

- to find a catholic school in which there is not an abject bowing to Modernism in the form of secular 'catechetics',
- or any school, in which there is not an equally abject capitulation to Humanism in the form of explicit sex education,

in both of which Parents are singled out

- to be left in the dark as long as possible and afterwards
- for severe ridicule and criticism for daring to query and resist the 'total licence', the godless Humanists are demanding as the only good for their children,

Parents need reassurance

- that God is still completely in charge of world events;

- that it is still His Will to bring children into this apparent madhouse;
- that somehow it is still safe to do so;
- and that it is still possible to find one's road to Heaven by way of the Catholic Church.

In the face of the rampant Contraception Mentality, and the mounting pressure on all to comply with these 'lifestyles' for economic, social and health reasons, and in the 'deadly' silence that nowadays surrounds the Voice of *Humanae Vitae*, many Catholics and non-Catholics alike would like to remain reassured

- that the Church had God's Mind when She wrote that any form of Artificial Contraception is intrinsically evil,
- and consequently, that it is God's Will not to bar children from being born into the chaos of 'modern' living;
- *and that He will assist anyone who wants to obey his Laws.*

Fr. Kramer, in his fantastic book on the Apocalypse, *The Book of Destiny*, has shown with overwhelming evidence, that God wrote *a meticulous and meaningful record* in the Book of Revelation of St. John. This book contains *God's Official Account* of Who rules the world, and Who is in charge of the direction of world events.

In the face of the gathering strength of the claims by the humanists 'that their master Satan is to be hailed as the only alternative to God, to become universally accepted as the sole ruler of the world', God's Record is the Immovable Obstacle in the path of this revolt, and the book by Fr. Kramer is very timely indeed.

Following in the footsteps of this renowned Commentary by a great scholar, it is not merely my intention to highlight a unique ingredient: *The Dimension of Hope*, which is so clearly included in God's Final Record. This Hope is enshrined in a very special Person, a Person with a very special task in the History of the Church.

My book is about this Person
"Hail, Holy Queen, Mother of Mercy,
Hail our Life, our Sweetness and our Hope …"

May all who read

The Marian Dimension in the Apocalypse of St. John

receive from 'the God of all encouragement' (Rom. 15:5) at least as much consolation as I received writing it, and please God even greater …

On the Feast of the
Immaculate Conception
of the Blessed Virgin Mary
Frits Albers, 1981.

Chapter One

What is Meant by the Marian Dimension

THE MARIAN DIMENSION *in history* is the development in time of the fulfillment of God's Promise in Paradise: the unrelenting, everlasting enmity "between the Woman and satan and between Her seed and his". This enmity and its ensuing struggle span the centuries and have their roots deep in the Old Testament, in the life stories of the holy Men and Women who together prefigure 'the New Israel' and 'the New Jerusalem': the Church founded by Christ in the New Covenant.

THE MARIAN DIMENSION *in the Apocalypse of St. John* is the epic of the gathering of 'Her seed', the Catholic Church, ever since She gave birth to its Head, Our Blessed Lord and Saviour Jesus Christ. If a woman started the defeat of Satan by being Immaculately Conceived, by believing the Word of God that came to Her in the message of the Angel, by freely giving Her consent to God's Divine Decrees for the Redemption of mankind and by giving birth to the only-begotten Son of the Father; then it is only fitting that it should be given to Her to partake in the completion of what Her Faith in God had begun: the gathering together of all those who, united with the Head of the Church, will in time resist the seed of Satan, which resistance, according to St. Grignion de Montfort, will culminate in the defeat of Antichrist.

Jesus Christ is undisputedly Mary's Seed from the Holy Ghost, and Jesus Christ is the Head of the Church He founded here on earth, to continue and complete His work of Redemption and the defeat of Satan and his seed. If this Church is modeled on His Holy Mother (Vatican II in *Lumen Gentium*), then all the members of this Church who are united to its Head, and all the Elect who thank their salvation to this Church, are as much Mary's Seed as they are united to Her Son. And it was by giving birth to the Head as well as to the members of His Body, that Mary was given the privilege and the honour by God of being "a cause of our salvation and of the defeat of Satan's seed".

The story of how the Mother of God was to carry out Her appointed role in time is reflected in the Marian Dimension of the Apocalypse of St. John. It is in the Book of Revelation that the story is unfolded of the gathering of 'Her Seed' as the partakers in Her victory: the victory of the Catholic Church over evil. For it is in the Apocalypse of St. John that the age-old Tradition of the Catholic Teaching: to see Our Blessed Lady as the Mother and the Model of the Church (St. Irenaeus), finds its Apostolic origin as well as its final unfolding. For in the Apocalypse Mary and the Church have become so inseparably one, that by Divine Decree and Inspiration they are being portrayed under the same imagery.

This should not come as a surprise to us, as the Book of Revelation is the work of the one to whom Our Blessed Saviour entrusted His most sacred possession: His Holy Mother. Not even the excruciating agony on the Cross in the dying moments of His life here on earth, could dampen Christ's Love for His Church, His Bride. When He gave His Mother to St. John, He entrusted to him the only teacher He ever had on this earth. And when He gave St. John to His Mother, He implored Her to teach the disciple all She had taught Him, and to share with the Apostle and future Evangelist the same incredible insights which the Holy Spirit had lavished on Her, His Bride.

That is how it came about that in the years they spent together the Marian Dimension within the Catholic Church and within the future history of the world became revealed to, and was finally understood by the beloved disciple in all its fullness: from the remote beginnings deep in the pages of the Old Testament until the final victory over Satan and his seed Antichrist, and even beyond …

The Gospels, and the theology of St. Paul, occupy primacy of place in the written records of our Redemption, yet the mystique of the Great Union between Our Blessed Lady and the Church founded by Her Son is there, in the sacred pages of Holy Scripture, to be discovered by all those who love Christ in His unique Bride, the Catholic Church. The Apocalypse may not be the most important book of Scripture, but we must never forget that without Our Lady and without Her unique Faith and Her obedient 'Fiat', there would never have been an Apocalypse, as there would never have been a Gospel, or a St. Paul or a St. John, or even a Saviour Jesus Christ. The use of the word 'dimension' may create the impression that a Christian can get by without the Blessed Virgin Mary, just as a man can 'get by' with only one eye; but according to God's Ordinance, Salvation and Redemption were uniquely and absolutely dependent on Her …

Furthermore, we do well to also remember that St. John even came to see Christ himself through the eyes of His Mother, as was most certainly intended by the Master. How much of this is reflected in the Fourth Gospel we may never truly know; but we do know for certain that the knowledge and understanding of Our Blessed

Lady surpasses even the comprehension of the 'beloved disciple'. And if the same 'Queen of Prophets' could predict in the Holy Spirit "that all generations will call me blessed", then it is not hard to fathom that God wanted 'the visionary of Patmos' to be enlightened and prepared by the same intimate conversations with Her who made the Father's Word Incarnate "increase in stature, in Wisdom, and in favour with God and man". [Lk. 2:52].

Mary, Mystical Rose, Ark of the Covenant. The unique, total, unreserved, exclusive and everlasting property of the Blessed Trinity ...

> "No first man ever grasped Her entirely;
> No last one will fully comprehend Her.
> For richer than the sea is Her knowledge,
> Richer than the great ocean Her comprehension."
>
> (Si. 24: 28-29)

Christ, as He appears to St. John in the first chapter of the Apocalypse in His truly unlimited Divinity, shining forth through His divinised Humanity, knows that His Sacred Humanity with all its benefits for the world would not have been there had it not been for the Faith and Love of His Mother. It was not that Grace and predilection had placed Mary into a position where it became impossible for Her to say 'NO' to God: God never works like that with His chosen instruments. For years Mary had been cooperating with undoubtedly extraordinary graces; but She would never have been seen and accepted as the '*Model of the Church*', if the Church had to struggle and battle to do God's Will faithfully and freely here on earth, while Mary, so to speak, 'had it made'. VATICAN II clearly teaches that it was the doctrine of the Church right from Apostolic times: "that Mary cooperated in an altogether singular way '*as the New Eve*'." Her holiness was not a passive gift from God, but something She too had to carve out painstakingly from the circumstances of Her life: from the most minute to the most sublime, from the tranquil and joyful all the way to Calvary. It was for this that Christ could entrust to Her the formation not only of the disciple He loved, but even more so of the Bride He loved.

This is very profound for once again it presupposes Our Blessed Lady's active cooperation with the new work, a new 'Fiat' for '*the added dimension …*'. And it was precisely this knowledge of Our Lady: *that once again She freely accepted Her role in the Church founded by Her Son*, which became known to St. John, and which became 'THE MARIAN DIMENSION' in the final book of the New Testament: the Book of Revelation.

If this great Book of Destiny unfolds for us the struggle of the Church with the powers of darkness in time, and if God in the only official text of Sacred Scripture accepted by the Catholic Church, the Vulgate of St. Jerome, says: "… et *ipsa* conteret caput tuum …", "… and *She* shall crush your head …", and if St. Louis Grignion de Montfort tells us that the final fulfillment of this First Prophecy will consist in the defeat of Antichrist; then the history of the Catholic Church in her struggle to overcome the power of Satan must *of necessity* have a Marian Dimension, which must be clearly reflected in the prophetic Book officially dealing with that struggle and its hard-won victory.

If in the Apocalypse of St. John Our Blessed Lady and the Catholic Church founded by Christ have become inseparable, portrayed as they are by the same imagery, then the solicitude of the one reflects the concern of the other, and the care with which the Catholic Church gathers together God's children from the four corners of the globe is the surest sign of the Marian Dimension at work in the world, by which the Holy Mother of God gathers together Her seed, as God predicted She would, in union with Christ, the Head, and to His everlasting Glory.

With ever greater clarity, then, it is becoming increasingly more clear that all who are at present engaged in spreading devotion to Our Lady at this advanced stage of a second corruption of humanity, are urging people once again to *enter into the Ark of God* to be saved once again from a Second Deluge: a deluge of Sin and Evil, which will engulf the globe at the time of Antichrist. Like in the days of Noah, we once again have a clear choice: to enter the Ark, or to swim and struggle as best we can outside. To enter into the Church of which Our Lady is the Model and of which Her Son is the Head, or to remain on the outside. To let Our Lady 'gather us up' and carry us safely over the corruption of our days to the fullness of Christ's Redemption, or to 'follow the world in running after the Beast'. (Rev. 13: 9).

We can be sure of one thing: the first choice will be to the Glory of God and our own delivery; the second will be at our eternal peril. One will lead to an even greater manifestation of the honour, the power and the Love of Our Blessed Lady before 'the full Assembly' of God, the Church, and before all the nations on earth, to the everlasting Glory of the Most High.

The other will lead to enslavement …

Chapter Two

Some Aspects of the Marian Dimension

The world of our times seems to have come into the grip of forces of such global magnitude that they produce changes which have the distinct appearance of being inexorable. Ordinary people are left to cope with both the forces and the changes with means which are proving more and more inadequate and futile by the day, resulting in effects which run from belligerence and anger, through frustration and profound anxiety all the way to escapism.

As is to be expected, many analyses have been made of this stark phenomenon. Depending on the analysts' 'philosophy' and grasp, these studies range from the utterly useless and superficial to those which strike us as profound and acceptable. The great majority of the more popular descriptions of our plight confuse causes and effects, and propose the more immediate and obvious symptoms as the reasons for the malaise. For example, one widely accepted slogan tries to tell us that 'bad television' is a cause of our slide into the world's unhappy state. But such a cliché obviously ignores the more fundamental reasons: (a) why 'bad television' should be *produced* in the first place, and (b) why 'bad television' should be *accepted.* Neither the *production* of 'bad television', nor the *acceptance* of it are explained by such an easy generalisation, since it refuses to explain, e.g., why 'bad television' has no effect on a lot of other people.

Gradually, then, the more thoughtful people amongst the students of the modern breakdown of society are veering away from pointing to the more popular 'material' causes, such as 'television', 'affluence', 'materialism', 'permissiveness', 'technology', as they consider them inadequate to explain the profound changes that are taking place everywhere, even in man himself. And they will argue that we will have to look for other more deeper causes, which they, sometimes to their great distress, are forced to label 'spiritual', to distinguish them from the others.

From the welter of literature available on this subject, we may start to isolate some common denominators, by which the aforementioned more thoughtful analysts tend to agree with one another.

Many see it as a '*values-revolution*'. Old values are no longer acceptable, newer ones are feverishly looked for and even created. Since this cannot be done by individuals-in-isolation, groups (be they crowds, hordes, mobs, terrorists, guerillas, militant unions, teams) are everywhere forcing their wills over existing formations and institutions to make them accede to their demands, which make the occupants of these traditional 'corridors of power' seem powerless and unfaithful even to themselves which, in turn, accelerates their own demise and their replacement by more radical elements: the creation of a new society. Although the onslaught ['struggle' is too mild a word for it today] has been lifted from a material battlefield to a more 'spiritual' one, one of values, power and the mind of men, the main question is still not answered: *why* the mass-abandonment of cherished values? *Why* the global exodus from the known, the trusted, the tried, not by a handful of surrealist artists, religious iconoclasts and avant-garde 'educators', but by the suburban housewives, the children and even the aged ...?

Part of the answers to these bewildering questions are provided by Harold J. Laski in his book: *The Dilemma of our Times* (1952, George Allen and Unwin Ltd., London), when he analyses for us the 'law': "*All revolutions relax the inhibitions of civilised living*", (p. 177f). Which means that, if there is widespread selfishness, rudeness, insolence, violence, brutality, immorality, which are all signs of a 'relaxation of inhibitions of civilised living', then this could be pointing to a worldwide revolution.

Alvin Toffler in *Future Shock* goes one step further, and declares all this the symptoms of a *sick society*:

> "A revolution shatters institutions and power relationships. This is precisely what is happening in all the high technology nations. Students in Berlin and New York, in Turin and Tokyo, capture their deans and chancellors, bringing great clanking education factories to a grinding halt and even threaten to topple governments. Police stand aside in the ghettos of New York, Washington and Chicago as ancient property laws are openly violated. Sexual standards are overthrown by young and old. Great cities are paralysed by strikes, power failures and riots. International power alliances are shaken. Financial and political leaders secretly tremble – not out of fear that communist (or capitalist) revolutionaries will oust them, but that the entire system is somehow flying out of control.

> These are the indisputable signs *of a sick social structure*, a society that can no longer perform even its most basic functions in the accustomed ways. We are simultaneously experiencing a youth revolution, a colonial revolution, an economic revolution, and the most rapid and deep-going technological revolution in history." (p. 172).

What Harold Laski still thought of as simply a 'relaxation', although admittedly brought about by adverse conditions, Alvin Toffler sees as the signs of 'degeneration', and is now subject to the brutal forces of the isolated chemicals, once kept in balance and bonded together to make one healthy compound, but now at war with each other because of loss of cohesion through decomposition.

Arthur Lyons in his book *Satan Wants You*, pursues the matter somewhat deeper again, and initially centres most of the upheaval around *truth*, and specifically *religious truth*. He writes:

> "Mr Hughes [Pennethorne Hughes, in *Witchcraft*, Penguin, 1967], missed the point when he said that only the resurgence of authoritarianism would bring back witchcraft in its old forms, for authoritarianism is not the catalyst that is needed to start the reaction. All that is needed is an interruption, a *BREAK*. Man is today undergoing a period of drastic change. A new world has suddenly dawned on him which he had not the foresight to prepare for … The old *religious forms* seem to have become insipid and irrelevant …

> *The truth of our existence has been tossed up for grabs* and men everywhere are grabbing in blind desperation." (p. 14).

We are now far removed from pointing the finger at isolated items like 'pornography' or 'television' as the prime causes for our downward trend. By his choice of words like 'catalyst', 'reaction', 'drastic change', Arthur Lyons too may sense the similarity of this downward trend with a chemical decomposition. But he is bringing in a new element, throwing light on a dark corner. By touching on the question of the *profound psychological changes in man himself* he is going away from the changes in society as being some irrational, brute and inevitable 'forces of nature' which repeat themselves every so often. Here we are told: *Man has changed the truth about himself. Man is changing himself. And everywhere, man is changing man.* And so the society in which he lived no longer fits him, suits him. And he breaks it apart. His bizarre taste for the lurid is now to be found within himself, and we may start to appreciate that the lurid, pornography, does not create its own market; but that the *lust* for it does. This lust as a symptom of a 'changed man', liberated from the 'inhibitions of civilised living', sign of a profound revolution indeed, [Laski], but now: *within himself.* Arthur Lyons again:

> "When man finds his accepted system of truth no longer significant, when he finds himself no longer relevant to his surroundings, *an acute crisis of identification follows.* [Quoting here the Spanish philosopher Ortega y Gasset, he continues]: The situation becomes critical, when man finds

> no solution in the normal point of view; his condition forces him then to hunt for an *escape* in a distant and eccentric extreme which formerly had seemed to him less worthy of attention.
>
> "When this gap between knowledge and culture widens altogether too much, man finds his existence jeopardised. He imagines that he can no longer turn to the system of knowledge within which he grew up, for it appears to him obsolete and no longer applicable to life. So he looks around frantically for something to get hold of, and for the duration of that span of time in which he finds himself left behind, and alone, *he is an outsider*, outside the bounds of society and its conventional morality." (p. 15).

Having brought us face to face with the root-causes of the universal distress: the psychological changes brought about by man himself inside himself, because of the profound *CHANGE IN THE TRUTH ABOUT HIMSELF*, Arthur Lyons then draws our attention to some very basic consequences of this harrowing process, when he writes:

> "The individual who finds himself unprepared for such a situation, who is unable to turn inward to find stability [during his spell as an uncomprehending, impotent outsider], such a man experiences uncomfortable feelings of acute futility and inadequacy. *He wants to reassure himself; he needs to reassert himself.* In trying to overcome these acute disorders (disorientation), in order to find meaning in his

> seemingly aimless existence, man searches for ways *to manipulate his environment*, in order to demonstrate to himself and to others his dominance over the external realm. In its present political and social forms, this tendency takes on violent overtones …"

Here we are told that that isolated chemicals (factions), which once formed the compound 'society', are attracting the disoriented and disillusioned individuals of their choice. People join the groups which better express 'the new truth' they found about themselves, or the new 'identity' they have adopted; or, more likely, the ones they think will dominate the other breakaways from society: IRA, Communists, Neo-Nazis, PLO, Maoists, witches, satanists, Humanists, Mafia, Freemasons …

> "But more interesting then these (political and social changes) are the changes that are occurring beneath the surface, within the character of man himself. These changes are more subtle than those brought about by physical violence, although in some of their more ominous forms they too do entail violent action of some sort. [COERCION!]. They are all part of an integrated pattern: *A QUEST FOR POWER* … This particular, more individual, usurpation of power claims for itself the complete licence to 'go down streets' previously denied to all but the most dedicated, for it entails a search into dark and mysterious secrets …"

If changes in man himself have caused the slow and agonizing dissolution of society, the break-up of society itself forces isolated and estranged individuals to group together as 'molecules' in the warring 'chemicals' for the most basic aim: power, power to dominate, to 'survive'.

This will do to extract the most essential details from the serious attempts being made here to unravel for us the baffling turn of events human history has taken even in our own lifetimes.

1. "*A deep psychological change*" in man himself, caused by a change *in the truth about man*. Here we think mainly of *evolution* which changed man from being created 'in the image and likeness of God' into an 'evolved animal' with animal ancestors. No wonder he feels himself 'free' to fight other 'animals' in times of scarcity. (Survival of the fittest!)
2. "*The Identity Crisis*", which must follow the profound change in the concept of man, making society into a jungle in which live all the other 'evolved animals'.
3. "*The Quest for Power*", needed after the identity crisis as a means for self-reassurance and self-assertion, and also to dominate the environment, and to survive in the 'jungle'.
4. "*Escapism*" for all who cannot identify with a particular group ('chemical') during the slow process of dissolution of society.
5. "*Community*" the final arbiter. For most who suffer from an 'identity-crisis', the 'community' is the particular 'chemical', 'power-group' they have joined and identified with. The rules and 'laws' of that group become the final authori-

ty the individuals recognise. But since such groups mainly consist of people who do not really know who they are or why they live, and who joined their particular group out of convenience more than out of conviction, the cohesion is not strong, and the majority remain drifters. The result will be a global *collectivism*: the goal of all communism.

The Catholic Scene

By now the astute reader will have come to realise why the foregoing had to be brought up at all, and was analysed with a certain amount of detail. For the description given there fits not only the secular world of our time, in which the Catholic Church has to fulfill Her allotted task: the salvation of souls. It fits even more alarmingly the struggle-to-death the Church is at present waging with Her arch-enemy: *Modernism*, in which brutal war *the Marian Dimension* has to play its decisive role. Since this book is about 'The Marian Dimension', we must link it to the Catholic situation first.

If, as we saw, *evolution* has drastically changed secular man's concept of himself, *Teilhardian Evolution, i.e. Systematic Modernism*, has caused the collapse of Catholic Faith in thousands upon thousands of adherents. *It has changed the Truth about Catholic Man!* Consequent upon that, it has caused the greatest *crisis of identity* amongst modernist bishops, priests, nuns, brothers, lay people, and 'theologians' the Church has ever known.

In accordance with the above-developed analysis, these unfortunate catholics have banded together for some 'reassurance' in a distinct group. To reassert themselves, to wield their collective dominance over the Body of Christ to change it according to their own 'image and likeness', they use all the evil means Secular Humanism has put at their disposal: *coercion, ostracism, ridicule and derision of the faithful, compulsory indoctrination through sensitivity training, group dynamics and other brainwashing techniques used by the enemy – notably in enforcing a humanist 'catechetics' and an intolerable classroom sex education on Catholic children under their charge.*

They have caused a revolution in the Church, and, like with all revolutions, the ensuing break-down in Church discipline 'has relaxed the inhibitions of a vast majority of other catholics' (Laski), eager to do their own thing without yielding altogether to the Modernism of the others.

'Truth is up for grabs' (Arthur Lyons) in the 'catechetics', 'theology' and 'philosophy' that emanates from these polluted sources.

'Community' is their catch-cry, the 'base communities' formed everywhere to replace parishes or decent family living. Is it any wonder that the only name fit to describe these 'agglomerates of walking identity crises', is the one given to them by a far-seeing Pontiff in 1910, Pope St. Pius X: "*the 'church' of darkness ...*".

To this 'church' must be given – according to this very same Saint and Pope – the description of St. John in the 13th chapter of the Book of Revelation: a world-wide anti-church '*that looks like the Lamb but speaks like the Dragon*, doing everything in its power to bring the world under the tyranny of the first Beast ...'.

And with this we have returned to the central subject-matter of this book. For this 'church', this teilhardian agglomerate, this modernist 'community', *is the gathering of Satan's seed* for the final assault on the Catholic Church, to be resisted and crushed by the Woman of Genesis, the Woman appointed by God for that task: Our Blessed Lady, and by '*Her Seed*': Our Lord, and the Church He founded, of which He is the Head, and She is the Mother and the only Type and Model.

For a better understanding of what is to follow, we will once again turn to Arthur Lyons as quoted above, and we will re-write it here with suitable modifications as follows:

> "When a catholic finds his accepted system of Truths no longer significant, when he finds himself no longer relevant to his Church, [because of his fascination for Teilhard de Chardin e.g.], an acute crisis of identification follows.
>
> "The situation becomes critical when a catholic finds no solution in the orthodox point of view. His modernistic condition forces him to hunt for an escape in a distant and eccentric extreme: *evolution*, which formerly had seemed to him less worthy of attention.
>
> "When this gap between pseudo-knowledge and orthodox belief widens altogether too much, a catholic finds his existence in the Church jeopardised.
>
> "The individual who finds himself unprepared for such a situation, who is unable to turn inward *to his Catholic Faith* to discover stability, such a person experiences uncomfortable feelings of acute futility and inadequacy. He wants to reassure himself. He needs to reassert himself. In trying to get rid of these acute disorders (disorientation) so he can find some meaning in his seemingly aimless exist-

> ence as a catholic, he will search for ways to manipulate his catholic environment, in order to demonstrate to himself and to others his dominance over the *institutional Church* …
>
> "But of more interest are the changes that occur beneath the surface, within the very character of a catholic. These changes may be more subtle, but they are indeed drastic, and they are all part of an integrated pattern: *A QUEST FOR POWER!* This particular *catholic* usurpation of power claims for itself an unbridled licence to go down 'philosophical', 'theological' and 'catechetical' lanes previously blocked as incompatible with Catholic Faith; for they lead to no other 'dark and mysterious secrets' but the ones of Satan's '*church of darkness*'…". (End of modified quote.)

Having made this analysis, we are at last in the position to do justice to the title of this Chapter Two. What are some of the aspects of 'The Marian Dimension'? Of this gathering of 'the Woman's Seed' in opposition to 'Satan's seed'? For that something is to be done about this rampant global evil, is obvious.

For a start, Modernists no longer recognise and acknowledge the Catholic Church *as their Mother*. They no longer see themselves *as Her children*. Like in the dissolution of secular society described in these pages, where people in the grip of a profound change of the truth about their own existence and that of the society in which they live, dissociate themselves from their parents and families, to adopt surrogate ones, so also do the teilhardian modernists turn on the Church, uproot their Catholic existence, and find themselves equally forced to adopt a second-rate 'spiritual mother': 'the church of darkness', and a new, fictitious origin and lineage: '*evolution*'.

A MOTHER, therefore, seems to be at the heart and centre of every potential identity crisis, either to forestall one as the familiar and stabilizing influence, as the trusted rock of security, as the solid ground in which the roots are firmly planted, and as the faithful echo responding to the cries of anguish thrown up at her from life's dark valleys; or else she is the last point from which the anchor lines of life are finally being severed … And if that is true for everyday life, it is equally true for the tortuous road to Eternity.

Man is changing; changing himself, changing others. But no matter what changes, he knows whose child he is and who brought him into the world. And he knows from whom he will have to cut himself loose, if he wants to change the truth about himself … And here we see God's psychology for mankind in general *and for our Holy Mother the Catholic Church* in particular. For here is where Our Lady, a Mother, comes in: a Catholic does not change if he remains Her child! He will not change himself or others. Love for Our Lady was meant by God to forestall a break with the Church! And in that way a child of Mary will not only remain a child of the Father in Heaven: he will have no trouble accepting this as *THE GREATEST, EVERLASTING, UNCHANGEABLE TRUTH ABOUT MAN!* Love for Our Lady wipes evolution: *that change in the Truth about man that has caused so much havoc!*

God's ideal solution to stop the dissolution of society and the erosion from the Church must include a mother, THE MOTHER, for She stops any change in this fundamental Truth about man himself. And with that, God's Solution will prove the most enduring, the most stable, the most 'bonding' and the most resistant to decomposition. The Marian Dimension, as the extension of Mary's Motherhood, fits perfectly these requirements.

So this seems to be what God had in mind when He revealed to St. John the existence of 'The Marian Dimension' in human history, and when He let the greatest manifestation of that Dimension coincide with the greatest deployment of Evil. It provides a solution which is at once TRUE, POWERFUL, COMPATIBLE with the Catholic Church, and with its ROOTS deep in the Old Testament.

We will take this last aspect first.
For She is a breath of the Majesty of God,
Pure emanation of the glory of the Almighty,
Hence nothing impure can touch Her.
She is the reflection of the Eternal Light,
Untarnished mirror of God's active Power,
The image of His Perfection.
Although alone, She can do all,
Herself unchanging, She makes all things new.
In each generation She enters into holy souls,
Forming them into friends of God and prophets.
For God loves only those who live with Wisdom.
She is indeed more splendid than the sun.
She outshines all the constellations.
Compared with light, She takes precedence.
For light must yield to night,
But over Wisdom evil will never triumph.

She deploys Her strength from one end of the earth to the other,
It is She who orders all things for good …

[Book of Wisdom, 7:25-8:1].

Alone I encircled the vault of the sky,
And walked the deep of the abyss,
The waves of the sea, the whole earth,
To reveal My power to every people and nation.
Among all these I searched for a rest,
An inheritance where I could remain.
Then the Creator of all gave Me His command,
And He who wrought Me, decided the place for My tent,
And He said, 'In Jacob will be Your abode, make Israel Your inheritance'.
And thus I became established in Zion.
He made Me live in His beloved city,
In Jerusalem is My dominion.
This I took root in a privileged people,
In the Lord's property, in the midst of his inheritance.

[Ecclesiasticus 24:8-16].

With these inspired words, the Holy Authors extol the incomparable beauty of Created Wisdom. And by introducing Her as speaking, and as addressing us, they clearly mean to impress upon us *to think of Wisdom as a person, someone who teaches us*. The whole becomes one ardent prayer of longing for the Redemption in Jesus Christ, the Eternal Wisdom.

But in applying these Sacred Texts from time immemorial to Our Blessed Lady in the Liturgy on the trustworthy example of the Fathers and Doctors of the Church, the Holy Catholic Church has acknowledged that the holy people of the Old Testament, in calling for a Redeemer, *were also calling for Her* who has been elected from all Eternity to be His Mother. And so these inspired and sacred texts *on Created Wisdom* also extol Her who has shown such great wisdom in trusting God, letting Her unbounded Faith in God become a sure beginning of our Redemption.

The above quoted words show unmistakably therefore that *the Marian Dimension* has its roots planted firmly in the Old Testament; starting with the First Prophecy by God in Genesis, and carried through in the longing and the prayers and actions of God's people: Israel.

A few comments to link these two passages of Holy Scripture with what we have said before.

- ❖ The magnificent beginning introduces Wisdom, not as equal to God, but as a reflection of God: as created. Yet, the whole is a very powerful reference to the Immaculate Conception of Our Blessed Lady, which makes Her alone and unique amongst all other creatures. The thoughts of Her come naturally and easily, as, no doubt, intended by the Holy Spirit.
- ❖ "Although alone, She can do all …" Through the Incarnation Our Lady has allowed God the Son, our Redeemer, to touch us all with His Humanity. Wherever He is, She is

there with Him as the 'New Eve', undoing the 'knot of Eve', right up to our times …

- "She deploys Her strength …", etc. The Incarnation, brought about through Her unreserved 'Fiat' ('Let it be done'), has reached from one end of the earth to the other. Once that 'Fiat' was given, it was through Her 'that all things were ordered for good …'
- "Alone, I …" As already remarked, the Immaculate Conception and Her desire to use it for the plans God had for the Redemption of the whole human race, have made Our Lady stand alone before God with Her momentous decision. Here, Wisdom is depicted in its desire to share with others this glory and power which is inherent in such a magnificent creature of God.
- "Thus I took root in a privileged people …" The 'privileged people' of the New Testament, the Catholic Church, prefigured here by the old Jerusalem and the old Israel. No other christian church wanted Her …
- "To reveal My power …", "She deploys Her strength …" As we have seen: the break-aways, the revolutionaries, the modernists WANT POWER. They want to reassert themselves, showing everybody how 'powerful' they are in manipulating their environment. If only they knew how puny their make-believe 'power' is, and where the *real* power lies … Right here in the Catholic Church, with Our Blessed Lady for Mother.

When Christ was reduced to immobility, nailed to the Cross, He was, at that very moment, *the most powerful Man on earth*: alone redeeming the whole human race. And the annihilated, crucified Church of our times is a Church in love ... *And a Church in love is the most powerful Force on earth: irresistible ...*

And of *that Church* Our Blessed Lady is the Mother and Model. No other church wanted Her; no other church welcomed Her; no other church reveres Her, loves Her, prays to Her: least of all the break-away 'church of darkness' ...

1. The Marian Dimension has *STABILITY*.

   With its roots deep in the Old Testament, it has thousands of years of Tradition, guaranteed by God himself, Who wrote the inspired pages. And with an unbroken lineage in the Catholic Church, its future is secured. For 'the gates of hell will never prevail over the Rock of Peter', nor over the Church built upon that Rock, of which Our Blessed Lady is the Mother and Model.

2. The Marian Dimension is *TRUE*.

   Of the 'first woman' St. Paul wrote to Timothy in 1 Tim. 2:14:

   "Adam was not deceived, but the woman was deceived and so became a transgressor".

The Marian Dimension centres around the Woman who, Heaven and Earth can testify, was never deceived when She listened to the message of the Angel and gave Her consent. There is no deception anywhere around Her. 'But over Wisdom, evil will never triumph …!' Whoever loves Her, prays to Her, follows Her, will never be deceived, never be led astray, never miss finding 'the fruit of Her womb, Jesus'.

The Marian Dimension centres around a 'second Fiat', by which She who gave Her First Fiat in so much Faith, Love and Obedience, now also has consented to be the Mother of the Mystical body of Christ (St. Paul) as well as of the Head. This second Fiat is as void of deception as Her first Fiat, may it also be as fruitful …

3. The Marian Dimension is *POWERFUL.*

It will crush Satan's head. It will never allow anyone, entrusted to Her care, to be taken from Her protection. No one who wants to 'rule the world' will have cause to go away from Her …

4. The Marian Dimension is a *MOTHER.*

No one identified with Her will ever suffer a 'crisis of identity'. She will always recognise Her children. They will always know Her as their Mother.

5. The Marian Dimension is *COMPATIBLE WITH THE CATHOLIC CHURCH*

Without it, the Church would be at a loss. She would suffer a 'crisis of identity', for She would have lost Her Mother and Her Model.

Through 'the Marian Dimension', the Catholic Church knows *how* to be what she is supposed to be by Christ's Institution: the Bride of the Lamb of God, the Mystical Body of Christ, the Mother of the Elect: our Holy Mother, the Catholic Church.

Chapter Three

Roots and Development of the Marian Dimension: The First Three Chapters of the Apocalypse

Introduction

The first three chapters of the Book of Revelation form a distinct unit on their own. On the stage is the imposing figure of Our Lord and Saviour, Jesus Christ, the undisputed Ruler of the world, the unchallenged Head of His Church. He is alone; He says what He has to say, and He dictates what has to be done. Without interference, interruptions or arguments. His vision spans the centuries, from the remotest past to the most distant future. Here we are truly in the presence of God-made-Man.

The first chapter is made up of 20 verses, which between them count 16 references to the Old Testament, listed by the Jerusalem Bible. The second chapter has a total of 29 verses with 17 listed references, whereas chapter three has 22 verses with 36 listed references. The first three chapters of the Book of Revelation, therefore, consist of a total of 71 verses, which between them contain the impressive number of 69 listed references to the Books of the Old Testament. This can be no coincidence. Christ is obviously using His authority here to explain Sacred Scripture. By directly referring to 69 passages of the Old Testament, sometimes even quoting them verbatim, He makes it clear how some of the Old Testament is to be understood in the context of the New Testament. He does not mean to exhaust the meaning of the Old, but we may not quarrel with the special understanding He himself gives here to some of the passages of the Old Testament in order to shed light on the New Testament: His Light, Supernatural Light.

From these quotes, and with the aid of the Light He attaches to them, it must be possible to gain a better understanding of the opening and the initial thrust of the last Book in the entire Bible.

To facilitate research in these matters, I have printed in full, and attached to each chapter of the apocalypse as it is dealt with in this book, all the Old Testament references as they appear in chronological order in each chapter. To have the Old Testament texts before them, side by side with the appropriate page of the apocalypse whenever reference is made to these either by the holy Author or by this commentary, must be of great assistance to the readers in the arduous task of coming to grips with the technicalities, let alone the meaning, of this difficult Book. St. John seems to encourage this research: in fact, like a good teacher, he holds out a prize 'for the best student' when he writes in v.18 of Ch.13: "There is need for shrewdness here: if anyone is clever enough, he may interpret the number of the beast …". In other words, we are encouraged, even invited, to do our 'homework'. And much of this 'homework' is done in the pages of the Old Testament, hence my endeavors to put this groundwork at your disposal. If for no other reason then to show the richness and the cohesion of the Word of God.

Some Biblical Considerations

The New and Old Testaments form one unbreakable bond, one organic unit. The Word of God is but One. As was already made clear by the Author Himself: "Not one iota will be changed". And, "My Words will not pass away". [Mt 5:18; Lk 21:33].

One major asset of Fr. Herman B. Kramer's commentary on the Apocalypse: *The Book of Destiny* (Tan Books, 1975) is, that in it he has gathered a massive dossier of explanations of Old Testament imagery used in the Apocalypse. His work is indispensable for any serious student of St. John's Book of Revelation. This means that, if the MARIAN DIMENSION, [on which Fr. Kramer is completely silent!], is an integral part of God's Inspiration in the composition of the Apocalypse of St. John, then the roots of this must be equally present in the Old Testament as clearly and convincingly as the rest of God's Message. So that the Marian Dimension can grow organically from the Old Testament into the New Testament, and from the New Testament, through the Apocalypse, into the future Life of the Church here on earth.

As is already sufficiently known, God revealed the Marian aspect of the future Redemption of the human race in the First Book of the Bible, the Book of Genesis, when, according to God's Prophecy and Promise, after the Fall of our First Parents, the unrelenting enmity between the Woman and Satan, and between Her Seed and his, would finally end with the Woman crushing the head of the accursed with Her heel.

This shows the importance God attaches to Secondary Causes in the work of Redemption and Salvation, and to the Marian aspect of this work.

If now in the story of the Last Book of the Bible, i.e. in the Book containing the unfolding in time of all the aspects of the final struggle in this global and everlasting enmity, "The Woman" reappears, then we cannot dismiss this as a 'literary form' used by St. John, since God, the Author of the scenario, not only placed a Woman at the beginning of the story, but also foreshadowed that She would carry the victory in the end.

If in time the Catholic Church will gain the final and crushing victory over Antichrist, Satan's most renowned seed, modeling Herself on Her great model and mother, Our Blessed Lady, to whom God referred in Genesis, then mother and Church are indistinguishable in their enmity towards, their struggle with, and their final victory over, Organised Evil. These then are the Secondary Causes, willed by God in support of the Lamb of God, the First and the Last Cause, the Beginning and the End of everything …

And then it will not be hard to see how slowly, over the centuries, the "heel" of the woman is made up of Catholics who have understood and appreciated the deep affinity between Our Blessed Lady and the Church, and so have developed and maintained a singular devotion to the Mother of God. If it is through those Catholics that in the Age of the Great Apostasy the victory of the Church over Evil is finally obtained, and if these Marian Catholics received their whole inspiration and strength from the Blessed Eucharist and from the hidden fullness the Catholic Church receives from this Abiding Presence of Her Founder and Head, then it is

Christ Himself Who, through His Church, has inspired those Marian Catholics to model themselves in this unique way on His Holy Mother.

Christ, His Mother, and His Bride, the Catholic Church, are in perfect and everlasting unity, at the same time that each is a distinct and unique cause of that victory over Antichrist: Satan's main and final seed. All three are playing their very own role in this struggle through time, culminating in a Second Struggle to Death, not unlike the First One, the one on that very first Good Friday, culminating in the Death of the Second Adam, and the 'almost death' of the New Eve, giving birth to us, Her sinful children, to Eternal Life gained by Her Son on the Cross.

And although it is clearly understood and stated here, that most of what is to follow can be applied with equal validity to the Catholic Church, because of the unbreakable bond between mother and children, and between Model and duplicate, we may allow our attention to be directed in the following pages to God's first and foremost handiwork: the Immaculately Conceived Mother of His only-begotten Son; and we may rightly call this distinct and unique existence and activity *THE MARIAN DIMENSION IN THE APOCALYPSE.*

Section 1

The First Chapter in the Book of Revelation

We are in the presence of Christ. St. John knew Him intimately. He had lived with Him for three years. He had obtained great, even mystical, sanctity. Yet, even he, the 'disciple Jesus loved', fell 'like dead' at the Lord's feet. And the quotes from the Old Testament attached to this first chapter will testify to it, that this is not an isolated occurrence. … Already in His appearance Christ directs our attention to the visions of the prophet Daniel, thus putting the final seal of His own authority on them: that they relate to Himself; making sure that we have them on hand now that He starts to reveal to us 'what is to come'. And what an appearance it is! It never fails to impress, even to overwhelm, the beholder.

Here is a Man in the fullest realisation that He is God. That 'all power has been given Him in heaven and on earth'. This is the same Man who once said: 'Unless you eat My flesh and drink My blood, you will not have life in you!' Who once turned to His Apostles and wanted to know: 'Would you like to go away too?' Who assured us that what He held in His hands was no longer bread, but His Body. And who, on another occasion, had told a mere creature: 'You are a Rock, and upon this Rock I will build My Church. And the gates of hell will not prevail against it …' These words stand forever, like all the other words spoken by this remarkable Man. For the speaker is also the Stone that dislodged itself from the top of a mountain and shattered the statue seen by the king in his dream, after which this Stone grew in size until it encompassed the whole world … [Dn 2:24, 35].

Nothing is excluded from this Man's universal dominion, nothing escapes His all-knowing attention. Everything is laid bare before Him. On the Cross He was our Redeemer, obedient unto death. Here He is the Victor, claiming His rightful inheritance. And part of that inheritance is that history, even the history of 'organised evil', will inescapably and inexorably have to serve Him and His ends.

From now on the centre of that history has shifted. Since His Death on the Cross, the centre of the whole Universe is the Church which contains His presence in the Blessed Sacrament of His Body and Blood. This Church, His Body in time, is, like His Human Body once was, subject to forces at work in His creation, but is not controlled by them. These forces cannot be fully understood in their true identity unless seen under a very special Light: the Light of Supernatural, Infused, Divine and Catholic Faith which He alone can give and communicate. The Light of this Faith will reveal to the possessor the true relationship between the Catholic Church and the rest of creation, and between the Head of this Church and all the other members.

Since God is the Author of both the Old and the New Testaments, *only ONE Church* was foreseen by, and could grow out of, the Revelation contained in the Books of the Old Covenant. And here, in the Last Book of the New Covenant, the Author, Christ, is at pains to make certain things clear to His beloved Church, the New and Spiritual Israel, inheritor of both the Promise and its fulfillment. No wonder, then, that central to the quotes, used by the Holy Spirit in the composition of the Apocalypse of St. John, are many of those, which in the Old Regime pointed beyond themselves and their immediate meaning to a higher one, the New Jerusalem of the future, foreseen and foretold by the Holy Prophets, but only fully understood by the Author Himself, Christ, the Second Person of the Blessed Trinity, the Word of God and Founder of the Church.

And now here we find ourselves in His Sacred Presence, overcome, like St. John, with awe, but also aware that next to our reverence, He requires from us a great and lasting love for that inestimable Gift of His: that Light of Catholic Faith, by which we can start to see and understand, that His Beloved Bride on earth, that new centre of history and the pivot in time around which everything revolves, that this Church of His has itself a Yardstick, a Rule of conduct, a Measure, a model and a Mother, *which surrounds it like an added dimension* in which the Church lives and breathes and feels at home. And part of the Divine Technique to reveal to us the existence of this Dimension is the special use Christ makes of the Revelation contained in the Old Testament to which the nature of the Marian Dimension can be traced back.

And with that assurance given, we know that our 'homework' is not the impervious task that it may have looked to us at first, when, approached under the superficial light of earthly curiosity, the Book of Revelation refuses to give up its secrets and remains closed to the curious in spite of its name, because of an irreverent and fleeting acquaintance.

The First Chapter, then, introduces Christ as the Son of God, in all the splendor of One 'who was, who is, and who comes', and in all the Royal Dignity of One who has conquered Death and Hell and is now conscious of the full and unlimited power this victory has bestowed on Him.

It also introduces His Humanity. It mentions His Death, and how He was pierced once for our sake. The vision describes His face, His hair, His Body, and the way it is dressed, His legs His sacred hands, His eyes … And with this, ever so delicately, this very first chapter introduces His Mother. This body, it was once formed inside Her. She used to dress it. The little hands, the tiny feet: She looked after them, and washed them clean, kissed them, when they were pierced for our sake, and we returned them to Her lap when they had done the task for which She had prepared them. … And now, while He is talking to St. John, She watches from the side, yet unseen, with a heart full of motherly pride and joy at the sight of Him, Her Son. The Queen behind this magnificent King!

The Holy Spirit once inspired St. Luke to write: "As for Mary, she treasured all these things and pondered them in her heart". (2:19). And: "His mother stored up all these things in her heart". (2:51). As before her, her forefather Israel had done. (Gen 37:11). The same Holy Spirit now inspires St. John to remind us of Mary and Her Wisdom already right at the beginning in the opening paragraph of the Apocalypse, v.3: "Blessed the man who reads this prophecy, and blessed those who listen to him *if they treasure all that it says*, for the Time is close".

The First Chapter introduces the Church. Right there where She is supposed to be: at the Saviour's side, even in His right hand. The Church, the Light of the world, the Star by which the nations and peoples on earth have to map their courses. This Church will appear under many more images as the story of the Prophecy gets under way; but the first one counts, and, like first impressions, always floats on the surface like a cork.

Finally, this First Chapter introduces Daniel, and the whole of the Old Covenant, to allow all the Holy Men and Women, who so faithfully laboured with God for its creation, to now inspire and strengthen those who, following in their footsteps, are called to suffer the same hardships for its fulfillment. The direct referral to the visions of the great prophet Daniel shows that, what he saw, had a meaning beyond the time of Antiochus Epiphanes, is still awaiting fulfillment in its major thrust, and is now going to be taken up by 'the Son of Man' of all times to be assigned its final role and meaning.

And we conclude with the observation made by Fr. H. Kramer, that there is method, and great order, and divine planning, and surprising originality in the whole of the Book of Revelation, which will reveal a magnificent historical chronology, as befits its Author, the Holy Spirit.

Old Testament References in Chapter 1

Dn 2:28. [p. 1425]. (v.1)

[Facing the king, Daniel replied, "none of the sages, enchanters, magicians or wizards has been able to tell the king the truth of the mystery which the king propounded]; 28 but there is a God in Heaven who reveals mysteries and who has shown king Nebuchadnezzar what is to take place in the days to come".

Ex 3:14. [p. 80]. (v.4)

And God said to Moses, "I Am Who Am. This is what you must say to the sons of Israel: 'I Am has sent me to you' ... This is my Name for all time; by this Name I shall be invoked for all generations to come".

Ps 89:27,37. [p. 874]. (v. 5)

And I shall make Him My First-born,
The most high for kings on earth.

Is 55:4. [p. 1231]. (v.5)

See I have made you a witness to the peoples,
A leader and a master of nations.

Ex 19:6. [p. 101]. (v.6)

"I will count you a kingdom of priests, a consecrated nation".

[which in conjunction with Rv5:10 reveals the TRUE RULERS of the world.]

Dn 7:13. [p. 1437]. (v.7)

"I gazed into the vision of the night. And I saw coming on the clouds of heaven, one like a Son of man.
He came to the One of great age And was led into his presence".

Zc 12:10,14. [p. 1541]. (v.7)

"... They will look on the one they have pierced,
and they will mourn for him as for an only son ..."

Dn 10:5-19. [p. 1442]. (v.13-15)

"... [and this is what I saw]:
A man dressed in linen, with a girdle of pure gold around his waist;
his body was like beryl,
his face shone like lightning,
his eyes were like fiery torches,
his arms and his legs had the gleam of burnished bronze,
the sound of his voice was like the noise of a crowd ...
I heard him speak, and at the sound of his voice I fell unconscious to the ground. I felt a hand touching me ...
When he had said these things to me I prostrated myself on the ground, without saying a word. Then someone looking like a son of man came and touched my lips ...

'Do not be afraid', he said, 'you are a man specially chosen; peace be with you; play the man, be strong'!"

Ezk 43:2. [p. 1415]. (v.15)

I saw the glory of the God of Israel approaching from the east. A sound came with it, like the sound of ocean, and the earth shone with His glory.

Jg 13:20. [p. 327]. (v.17)

As the flame went up heavenwards from the altar, the angel of Yahweh ascended in the flame in the sight of Manoah and his wife, and they fell face downwards on the ground. (Parents of Samson).

Ezk 1:28. [p. 1363]. (v.17)

[27 I saw him shine like bronze, and close to, and all around him from what seemed like his loins upwards, was what looked like fire;] 28 and from what seemed his loins downwards I saw what looked like fire, and a light all round like a bow in the clouds on rainy days; that is how the surrounding light appeared. IT WAS SOMETHING THAT LOOKED LIKE THE GLORY OF YAHWEH. I looked, and prostrated myself, and I heard a voice speaking.

Dn 8:18. [p. 1438]. (v.17)

[17 "Son of man", he said to me, "understand this: the vision shows THE TIME OF THE END"].

18. He was still speaking, when I fell senseless to the ground.

[19 … "Come", he said, "I will tell you what is going to happen when the wrath comes to an end; this concerns THE APPOINTED END"].

Is 44:6. [p. 1212]. (v.8,17)

Thus says Israel's king
And his Redeemer, Yahweh Sabaoth:
"I am the first and the last;
there is no other god besides Me …"

Is 48:12. [p. 1220]. (v.8,17)

"Listen to Me, Jacob,
Israel whom I have called:
I am the first,
I am also the last".

Dn 2:28. [p. 1425]. (v.1,19)

[See above].

Hab 2:2. [p. 1514]. (v.19)

Then Yahweh answered and said:
"Write the vision down,
inscribe it on tablets
to be easily read,
since this vision is for its own time only:
eager for its own fulfillment, it does not deceive …"

Section 2

The Second Chapter in the Book of Revelation
The First Four Letters

In the Blessed Eucharist Christ is the centre, the heart of His Church. His Church is completely known to Him, but He does not take over its role or activities. From the centre He loves, guards, guides and instructs His Church, but through the various organs

He Himself has created in Her to be His perfect Body in Time, for the duration of Her existence on earth until the End. His Church in Time, then, is the Centre of history; the Pivot around which everything else revolves and has its appointed position; the Fulcrum by means of which Forces are exerted which, in time, will dislodge and completely subdue all contrary forces; and the Chart by which everything else sets its appointed course and measures its adopted direction. Christ acts only through His Church …

And just as He began the Great Reversal of Human History from the protective Sanctuary of Mary's Womb, so now He completes His saving work from the Sanctuary of His Bride, enveloped by the same protection He enjoyed Himself: the one of the Marian Dimension.

These, then, are the ingredients of the next two chapters of the Apocalypse. Christ directing the affairs of His Church, but clearly depending on His Churches to carry out His directives in their local communities; and then, by carefully selecting His words, beginning the delicate task of laying the foundation for the *manifestation* of the Marian Dimension: the role of His Mother in fulfilling Her task allotted to Her by His Father's command in Paradise: the gathering of Her seed for the crushing defeat of Satan and his seed; the Epic of which is the central theme running through this remarkable Book.

Since the latter is the avowed purpose of this present work: drawing the reader's attention to the existence and manifestation of the Marian Dimension in the Apocalypse, it is humanly impossible to run a complete commentary on the whole of the Apocalypse as well. In any case, I would only duplicate the magnificent work already done so skillfully in this regard by Father Kramer. I can only try to give faithfully the briefest of summaries of his insights on each chapter, for the benefit of readers not in possession of his Commentary, adding to them my own thoughts on the enrichment of the material presented.

The general meaning of the text of chapter two is clear enough. Christ encourages the good done, brings out what is in need of correction and ends up each time with a reward for faithfulness and perseverance. The sins on omission: *allowing a lax state of affairs to drift on, out of a mistaken idea of charity*, (so prevalent these days) are not overlooked and are castigated. The letters, of course, could have been written to any Church in any diocese in the world at any time, and between them, together with the ones in the next chapter, provide a comprehensive picture of what a Bishop, who wants to pursue 'what is in the mind of Christ', must be on the look-out for.

The attached texts from the Old Testament support the general impression created by the Author. Christ's direct reference to the 'Balaam affair at Peor' shows that the severity of the Old Testament's *condemnation of idolatry* must have its counterpart in the New Testament in the grave concern of the Church over the fatal decision of *giving up the practise of one's Faith* because of the grave danger of *apostasy* in times of trial and persecution. That Our Lord had to point this out barely sixty years after His Death on the Cross shows that the danger is real and that the reasons leading up to it need constant and careful checking. That could be one reason why Our Lord wanted 'the Marian Dimension' to come to the notice of the young Church, so that the full benefits could be studied and become understood at a very early age.

In several places of His dictated letters in this second chapter, Our Lord made reference to His Mother, in line with what He had quietly set in motion in the first chapter.

Ephesus

The council of Ephesus, 431 AD, would never have been the success it was for the articulate debate on the Divine Maternity of Our Blessed Lady, had it not been for the groundwork Christ Himself had laid for the enlightened Faith in this popular Dogma here in Asia Minor. In His letter to the Angel of Ephesus, Christ dictated:

"To him that conquereth, I will give to eat of the tree of life, which is in the paradise of God."

In Patristic writings, this is universally accepted as a direct reference to Our Blessed Lady. The Garden of Eden, the earthly paradise, virginal soil, untouched by human hands, is but a pale reflection of Mary, the Paradise of God, the Secluded Garden in which He dwelt, untouched by any man, virginal soil of the Most High and unaffected by the universal curse of Original Sin. The 'Tree of Life' in this Paradise is, of course, Christ after the Incarnation.

The very first promise, thus, made by Christ for faithfulness, is a deep awareness, even understanding, of the intimate relationship *between Christ and His most Blessed Mother*. Devotion to Our Lady is not only Patristic, does not only have an Apostolic Origin: it is by

Divine Will and Promise. Revealed by Him who has the good of His beloved Church uppermost in mind …

Thyatira

The revelations made here by Christ with regard to the relationship *between His Holy Mother and His Church*, are so important and far-reaching that it is better first to quote His appropriate words in full:

> "But on the rest of you in Thyatira, all of you who have not accepted this teaching, or learnt 'the mysteries of Satan' as they are called, I am not laying any special duty; but hold firmly on to what you already have until I come. To him who proves victorious and who keeps working for Me until the end, I will give him power over the nations, and he will rule them with a rod of iron, as when earthen vessels are broken in pieces, as I Myself have received from My Father. And I will give him the Morning Star."

Once again, in Patristic literature, the 'Morning Star' is a name by which Our Lady is known. She is addressed by this name in the Litany of Loreto. The connection is clear: just as the morning star heralds in a new day prior to the rising of the sun, so the arrival of Our Lady heralds in the dawn of Our Redemption prior to the arrival of Christ, the 'Sun of Justice', [Mal. 4:2].

In mentioning the name 'morning star', Christ referred listeners and readers to the text of Isaias, 14:12, (attached), where the fall of another 'morningstar' is decried. It is applicable to any power that, in its pride, trusted only in its own strength, and so followed 'Lucifer' in his fall from the heavens. It is of course ultimately applicable to Antichrist, Lucifer's main seed. These people are only ironically referred to as 'morningstar': they did not announce any day break, no rising of any sun: they only announced themselves. For Christ there is only one Morning Star, THE Morning Star, His Mother.

With this, Christ here takes up the first prophecy in Paradise, for in this part of the Thyatira text, He mentions Satan directly by name, and His Mother by direct inference. He mentions the seed of Satan by name: those who are interested in 'the mysteries of Satan so-called', and the 'seed of the Woman': all those to whom He will give the Morning Star.

But there is much more: He dethrones Satan as the ruler of the pagan nations, and gives them into the power of those 'who will remain faithful to Him until the end, and for their reward get the Morning Star'. This means directly that His Church, on the example of His Holy Mother, trusting entirely on the powers of Her Divine Founder and Head, must be, and will be, a morning Star herself to all the nations, bringing to them the Sun of Justice unto Righteousness. His Church is made here and now 'the seed of the Woman', to fight Satan over the control of the nations, to dethrone him with the Divine Powers entrusted to Her and not to fear, but to welcome, *the Marian Dimension* extended to Her here for Her example and protection.

Through the clear link with the First Prophecy in Paradise, already made easier through His previous reference to 'God's Paradise' (Ephesus), Christ shows that the contents of this Prophecy:

the eternal enmity between the Woman and Satan, and between the Woman's seed and Satan's seed *is His Father's Will*, that His Father's Will is to be obeyed, as He carries it out here once again Himself, and that His Church is now the inheritor of the 'everlasting enmity' as well as of the final victory because of Her possession of the 'Morning Star': the same Woman about whom the Prophecy was made in the first place. No other 'church' would ever inherit this Woman, nor Her mortal enmity, not Her final victory ...

Old Testament References in Chapter 2

Gen 2:9. [p. 16]. (v.7)

Yahweh God caused to spring up from the soil every kind of tree, enticing to look at and good to eat, with the tree of life and the tree of the knowledge of good and evil in the middle of the garden.

Pr 3:18. [p. 936]. (v.7)

She (i.e. Wisdom) is a tree of life for those who hold her fast, those who cling to her live happy lives.

Is 44:6. [p. 1212], and (v.8)

Is 44:12. [p. 1220]. (v.8)

See these references in Chapter Three, Section I above.

Si 2:1. [p. 1038]. (v.10)

My son, if you aspire to serve the Lord,
Prepare yourself for an ordeal.

Dn 1:12,14. [p. 1423]. (v.10)

He (Daniel) said: "Please allow your servants a ten day trial, during which we are given only vegetables to eat and water to drink ..."

The man agreed to do what they asked and put them on ten days trial.

Nb 22:2. [p. 200]. (v.14)

Balak son of Zippor saw all that Israel had done to the Amorites, and Moab was seized with panic before this people because of their immense number. [Then follows the story of Balaam, son of Beor].

Nb 25:1-2. [p. 204]. (v.14)

Israel settled at Shittim. The people gave themselves over to debauchery with the daughters of Moab. These invited them to the sacrifices of their gods, and the people ate and bowed down before their gods. With Israel thus committed to Baal Peor, the anger of Yahweh blazed out against them.

Nb 31:8. [p 212]. (v.14)

They also put Balaam son of Beor to the sword ...

Nb 31:16. [p 212]. (v.14)

[15: Moses said: "Why have you spared the life of all the women?]. These were the very ones who, on Balaam's advice, perverted the sons of Israel and made them renounce Yahweh in the affair at Peor: hence the plague that struck the community of Israel ..."

Is 62:2. [p.1240]. (v.17)

The nations then will see your integrity,
all the kings your glory,
AND YOU WILL BE CALLED BY A NEW NAME,

one which the mouth of Yahweh will confer …
[4: but you shall be called 'My Delight',
and your land 'The Wedded' …]

Is 65:15. [p.1245]. (v.17)

But My servants are to be given a new name …

Jr 11:20+ [p. 1272]. (v.23)

But you, Yahweh Saboath, who pronounce a just sentence,
who probes the loins and heart,
let me see the vengeance you will take on them,
for I have committed my cause to you.

Jr 17:10 [p. 1281]. (v.23)

I, Yahweh, search to the heart,
I probe the loins,
to give each man what his conduct
and his actions deserve.

Ps 62:12. [p. 843]. (v.23)

… and you yourself repay man as his works deserve.

Ps 2:8-9. [p. 787]. (v.26-27)

Ask and I will give you the nations for your heritage
the ends of the earth for your domain.
WITH IRON SCEPTRE YOU WILL BREAK THEM,
SHATTER THEM LIKE POTTER'S WARE …

Is 14:12. [p.1165]. (v.28)

How did you come to fall from the heavens,
Daystar, son of Dawn?
How did you come to be thrown to the ground,
You who enslaved the nations?

[Story of the rise and fall of Antichrist, Lucifer's main seed, here foreseen and foretold].

Section 3

The Third Chapter in the Book of Revelation
The Last Three Letters

This chapter contains the most sinister: Sardis, the most sublime: Philadelphia, and the trouble in the middle: Laodicea

Sardis

The bishop of Sardis has the most ominous words in the whole of Scripture addressed to him: ***you are dead!*** They are on par with the foreboding of doom the Holy Evangelist attached to the departure of Judas from the Upper Room: 'Foras autem erat nox …'. Outside was the darkness of night … A 'night without end …'. Grace has stopped flowing through the bishop into his diocese. Consequently, the remark of the Saviour 'There are (only) a few in Sardis who have not defiled their garments …'. The brilliant white of these few faithful followers of the Lamb contrasts sharply with the blackness in the soul of their bishop. Except for these, the other names are about to be blotted out from the Book of Life.

This reference to 'blotting out', (as is no doubt the Great Teacher's intention), conjures up in the minds of His listeners the other places in the Holy Books where this expression has been used before. Notably in the 'prayer of Moses', in Ex 32:32, (attached), with its power of intercession. With the dire warning which these words most certainly contain, is therefore also expressed the fervent hope that, even more readily than in Moses' days, God will grant sinners repentance and pardon if others intercede for them, like Moses did, but now in the name of Jesus.

The whiteness of clothes, which in other parts of Revelation is directly related to *virginity*, must in the Mind of Christ have been closely related to the Virginity of His Holy Mother, and contains an exhortation to people in such perplexing circumstances, to take refuge in Her and not to lose heart, when they can no longer recognise the virginal Church in the laxity of the Clergy and faithful. The Laws of penance, fast and prayer (brought vividly back to mind by the example of Moses in Ex 32:32 through Christ's choice of words), must still be proclaimed and obeyed in spite of the worldliness of the bishop.

Philadelphia (St. Polycarp)

This is the only one of the seven letters from Christ, which does not contain a reproach. It is a beautiful 'certificate of merit' which does the receivers great credit. The letter radiates the warmth and compassion of its Divine Author. Here there is no shame attached to being 'totally known'. ...

Through their great and loyal fidelity, in inverse proportion to their numbers, a 'door' has been opened up to the whole country side of Asia Minor, and no one will be able to close it. This means that their missionary effect is irresistible. How highly Christ rates their powers of conversion can be seen from His remark that He will even bring Jews from the 'synagogue of Satan' under their influence, and that some of these will not only receive, but will also accept, the grace of true repentance and conversion.

With this, our Divine Saviour is bringing out yet another aspect of the *Marian Dimension.* He once compared Himself to 'the door of the sheepfold'. Yet, in His Divine omniscience, He also knows that the devout Catholic Tradition would pray to His Mother, and in the Litany of Loreto would address Her as the Porta Coeli: 'the Door of Heaven'. Because of Her powers of conversion for poor sinners who would take recourse to Her. The Marian Dimension is not only a protective shield, it is even more so a solicitous, energetic and *resourceful* Mother who is calling back Her children from the road to final ruin.

That Christ had His Beloved Mother in mind when He compared the missionary influence and activities of His faithful flock in Philadelphia with a door set open, becomes even more convincing, if we look at the rewards promised to the loyal pursuers of apostolic endeavours taken up on behalf of others. He will make them into 'pillars in the Sanctuary of His God, never to leave it'.

Through the Incarnation Mary became THE Sanctuary of God. Christ dwelt in Her as He now dwells in the Sanctuaries of Catholic Churches throughout the world. Mary became the Sanctuary of His Bodily Presence: the Sanctuary of God. To become a pillar in a sanctuary is synonymous with becoming one of the most important and lasting parts of a structure. All the furnishings are subject to change: they can be removed at will; but pillars cannot be taken away unless the whole structure is drastically altered. Here, then, the undertaking of an apostolate for the conversion of others on behalf of the Church, is rewarded with a unique devotion to Our Lady, which makes one ever more closely associated with Her, and adept in bringing others to the adoration of God in His Sanctuary.

Christ promises even more than this: He will personally write His mother's Name on these indispensable structures: these pillars. The name of the 'New Jerusalem'. For Mary was unique. She was to perfection, what God wanted His Holy People to be at least in willingness and in heart. She was the True, the New Jerusalem, the Beloved 'City of God'. She is also to perfection, what God wanted His Church to be, the New Jerusalem in Time. The new 'City of God' in Time.

With this, all the necessary aspects of *the Marian Dimension* have been completed. Christ, conscious of the relentless struggle His Church would wage with the powers of darkness, wanted His Church to have a 'sixth sense' for the presence of 'the Woman' His Father had first put in charge of that struggle, and to whom He had given the Divine Commission to 'beget children' in the likeness of the Promised Seed, His only Begotten Son, of Whom She became the Mother. Faithful to this command, which was not cancelled or nullified with the arrival of the Catholic Church, Mary now 'begets these spiritual children, Her seed', through the same Church through which Christ, the Head, works out the Salvation of the ages. To all the other aspects of this remarkable Church: the Papacy, the Sacramental system, the Priesthood, the Dogmas, of which understanding would grow in Time, but for which the foundations were laid by the Apostles, we must now also add 'the Marian Dimension'.

But with one difference, the final stroke of genius in the Divine Mastermind: the stamping of His Mother's Name on the pillars in His Father's Sanctuary!

Down the ages the Church would suffer the agony of break-aways from Her unity. These sects would build their own 'sanctuaries', claiming them to be the ones built by God. Something would be salvaged from the shipwreck which resembles some part taken from Mother Church. But unless Christ sees indelibly engraved into the pillars of the sanctuary the Name of His Holy Mother, He will not recognise the pillars, and will not consequently acknowledge the sanctuary as the one of His Father. Fervent, true, genuine, traditional and lasting devotion to His Mother, i.e. the acceptance of and glory in *the Marian Dimension*, will be recognised by Christ as the hallmark of the true Sanctuary of His Church. The prize for this can go to only one Church.

Old Testament References in Chapter 3

1S 25:29+ [p. 376]. (v.5)

"Should men set out to hunt you down and try to take your life, my Lord's life will be kept close in the satchel of life with Yahweh your God." (Abigail talking to David).

Ps 69:28. [p. 851]. (v.5)

"... blot then out of the book of life
strike them off the roll of the virtuous."

Ex 32:32. [p. 120]. (v.5)

"And yet, if it please you to forgive this sin of theirs! But if not, then blot out my name too from the book you have written."

Is 4:3. [p. 1148]. (v.5)

Those who are left of Zion
and remain of Jerusalem
shall be called holy
and those left in Jerusalem, noted down for survival.

Dn 12:1. [p. 1446]. (v.5)

"At that tine Michael will stand up, the great prince who mounts guard over your people. There is going to be a time of great distress, unparalleled since nations first came into existence. When that time comes, your own people will be spared, all those whose names are found written in the Book."

Ezr. 9:8. [p. 579]. (v.5)

"But now, suddenly, Yahweh our God, by His favour, has left us a remnant and granted us a refuge in His Holy Place; this is how our God has cheered our eyes and given us a little respite in our slavery. For we are slaves …."

Zp 3:13. [p. 1525]. (v.5)

…and those who are left in Israel
will seek refuge in the Name of Yahweh.

Against v.7 of this Ch. 3 of Revelations, the *Jerusalem Bible* makes two references in the margin in connection with the words 'the Holy and Faithful One': Lv 17:1 and Is 6:3, both with a + sign attached, meaning, that at the places referred to, more references can be found. The Old Testament abounds with references to the Holiness of God, and with His commands for holiness to His people. Since they are too numerous to be quoted here verbatim, here is a list of the places mentioned by the *Jerusalem Bible*:

Exodus	20:24	1 Samuel	2:2	Ezekiel	20:39
Numbers	4:15	Job	6:10		42:14
	10:10	Wisdom	5:19	Amos	4:2
Deut	12: 4-28	Isaias	1:4	Habakuk	1:12
Joshua	24:19		57:15		

Is 22:22. [p. 1176]. (v.7)

I place the key of the House of David on his shoulder;
should he open, no one shall close,
should he close, no one shall open.
I drive him like a peg into a firm place …

Is 45:14. [p. 1215]. (v.9)

Thus says Yahweh:
The peasants of Egypt and the traders of Cush,
And the tall men of Seba,
Will submit to you, and be yours;
They will follow you in chains.
They will bow down before you,
They will pray to you:
'With you alone is God, and He has no rival;
there is no other god'.

Is 60:14. [p. 1238]. (v.9)

The sons of your oppressors will come to you bowing,
At your feet shall fall all who despised you.
They will call you 'City of Yahweh',
'Zion of the Holy One of Israel'.
Though you have been abandoned,
And hated and shunned,

I will make you an eternal pride,
A joy for ever and ever.

Is 43:4. [p. 1210]. (v.9)

[I give Egypt for your ransom,
and exchange Cush and Seba for you].
Because you are precious in my eyes,
Because you are honoured and I love you.
I give men in exchange for you,
Peoples in return for your life.
Do not be afraid, for I am with you.

Is 49:23. [p. 1223]. (v.9)

Kings will be your foster fathers,
their queens your nursing mothers.
They will fall prostrate before you, faces to the ground,
and lick the dust at your feet.
You shall then know that I am Yahweh;
and that those who hope in Me will not be put to shame.

Zc 8:20. [p. 1536]. (v.9)

Yahweh Sabaoth says this. 'there will be other peoples yet,
and citizens of great cities ...'

Ezk 48:35. [p. 1422]. (v.12)

'The name of the city in future is to be: Yahweh-is-there'.

Jr 3:17. [p. 1255]. (v.12)

When that time comes, Jerusalem will be called: 'the throne of Yahweh'; all nations will gather there in the name of Yahweh and will no longer follow the dictates of their own stubborn hearts. [See also Is 1:26 and Zc 8:3].

Pr. 13:7. [p. 949]. (v.17)

There are some who, on nothing, pretend to be rich,
some, with great wealth, pretend to be poor.

Ho 7:9. [p. 1459]. (v.17)

[Ephraim mixes with the nations,
Ephraim is a half-baked cake].
Foreigners eat his strength away,
He is unconscious of it.

Ho 12:9. [p. 1465]. (v.17)

'How rich have I become!' says Ephraim,
'I have amassed a fortune'.
But he will keep nothing of all his profits,
Because of the guilt he has brought upon himself.

Is 55:1. [p. 1230]. (v.18)

O come to the water all you who are thirsty;
Though you have no money, come!
Buy corn without money, and eat,
and, at no cost, wine and milk.
Why spend money on what is not bread,
Your wages on what fails to satisfy? [See also Si 51:25].

Pr 3:12. [p. 936]. (v.19)

For Yahweh reproves the man He loves,
as a father checks a well-loved son.

Si 2:3. [p. 1038]. (v.21)

Cling to Him and do not leave Him,
so that you may be honoured at the end of your days.

Si 6:24-32. [p. 1043]. (v.21) Here is another translation:

But you, my son, put your feet into her fetters

and your neck into her harness.
Put your shoulders under her yoke and carry her,
and be not irked by her bonds.
Yes, approach her with all your soul
and keep her ways with all your might.
Go after her and seek her and she will reveal herself to you.
Once you hold her do not let her go,
for in the end you will find rest in her,
and she will be your joy.
Her fetters will be your strong defence …

Si 51:23f [p. 1110]. (v.18-21) [Here once again is another version.]

Come close to me, you uninstructed,
and stay for a while in my school.
For how much longer will you suffer the lack of all this,
While your souls are so thirsty for it?
Buy yourself Wisdom without money,
Bow your necks under her yoke,
Let your souls carry her burden.
She is never far from those who yearn for her,
And he who gives his soul to her will find her.
See for yourselves how slight my efforts have been,
And how great the peace I found in her …

Chapter Four

The Glories of the Church
Her Early Struggles and Victories
The Next Four Chapters of the Apocalypse

As already mentioned earlier, Fr. Kramer demonstrates with overwhelming evidence and learning, that the Book of Revelation is a painstakingly methodical book; as befits its Holy Author, the Holy Spirit of God. The chronological order through which he moves us in his commentary, *The Book of Destiny*, showing us the sights as in a vast panorama, is as mentally satisfying and stimulating as it is heart warming. Everything has its place and meaning; nothing is forced, artificial, contrived. But the Light of Faith is needed to see what is there: the Book remains closed and incomprehensible for the worldly curious.

Now that the Church has been founded and is taking firm root; Christ, in 7 letters to 7 Bishops in 7 Dioceses in Asia Minor, gives us a comprehensive insight into the things He will be looking for: the things He wants done and the things He finds reprehensible. For added security and for a sure guide in times of distress and uncertainty, He brought to the notice of the Early Church *The Marian Dimension* to remain with His Church for all times. He planted this special knowledge of, this love for, and devotion towards, His Mother as a seed in His Church; to be nurtured by the early Saints, cultivated by the Fathers and Doctors of the Church and enjoyed by future generations for the abundance of fruit to Eternal Life it would bring forth.

But in doing this, Christ was conscious of one other thing: *it was the Will of His Heavenly Father ...* As a reward for the faithfulness of Our Lady, and to ensure that Her genius in thwarting diabolical plans of the Evil One would not be lost, but would live on amongst the members of the Mystical Body of Christ, as surely 'Her children' as Jesus Christ, the Head, and would continue to inspire generations of Christians yet to be born.

As the story of the Apocalypse unfolds, then, we can expect the Marian dimension not to fade away as some pious practice; but to increase with the growing Church until the time that it can break out in all its glory for the defeat of Antichrist.

Section 4

The Fourth Chapter in the Book of Revelation
The Glory of the Church

What benefits has the establishment of the Catholic Church brought on earth? St. John, in two beautiful tableaux full of light, majesty and rest, is going to show us, before taking us into further Revelations of Her pilgrimage through the centuries. For it is for those benefits that the Church will have to struggle with the powers of darkness over who will rule the Nations. Future enemies will accuse Her of everything from political ambition down to seduction and deceit; and God in His Divine Wisdom wants to make sure that it will never be forgotten that the central mission of Her creation always will be: *to bring Heaven on earth.* God lives in Heaven. He also lives in the blessed Eucharist, where the whole of the Court of Heaven congregates to bring adoration, and invites the courts on earth to join in.

In 'routine' explanations of the text, I am letting myself be guided by the erudition of Fr. Kramer. According to him, then, we accept the following:

In the Book of Daniel [Dn 8:10], the Holy City is called 'the strength of heaven'; in the Hebrew text it is called 'the army of heaven'. Thus the Church of the Old Testament is called 'heaven'. Our Blessed Lord called His Church 'the Kingdom of Heaven'. In this place as in many others in the Apocalypse, St. John simply calls it 'heaven'. For further corroboration of this see Isaias 34:5, where God tells the prophet that His sword has been 'inebriated in heaven', meaning that it was drunk with the blood of the Jews, but would now turn also on their enemies. The simple word 'heaven' thus designates the Church, unless another meaning is clearly called for, and in the spirit, St. John here enters 'the Church'.

The fact that 'a throne was set in heaven' indicates that it is here not the eternal throne of God, but that of a Divine Institution. As the Judgements of God began at the Temple in the Old Testament, so they begin here at the Church. (See 1 Pet. 4:17).

In the New Order, God's Judgements will fall upon the nations for their disobedience, schisms, heresies, apostasies, infidelity and pride; for their hating and persecuting of the true believers and for leading them into vice. The Revelations will concern themselves directly with the work of Jesus Christ, with the work of Redemption. They will start from His Church, and will be depicted *as seen from God's viewpoint ...*

The blending of the two colours under which St. John sees the Divine Majesty, signifies the oneness of God's Holiness and Justice. The Rainbow is the symbol of His Mercy.

The '24 Elders' represent the Priesthood in the Church: participating in God's sovereignty (thrones), continually serving Him, working out His ordinances for the salvation of the people. They participate with Christ in His spiritual government.

God's Holiness manifests itself in a twofold guidance of the Church: Her endowments to spread the Gospel (lightning, voices, thunder) and His Divine assistance, or activity of the Holy Spirit (the seven lamps). Thunder being the voice of 'supreme authority'.

The 'crystal sea' is the laity. 'Sea' is often used in this type of literature for 'humanity', 'restless humanity', and so for 'upheavals, revolutions, commotions'. [The 'beast' rising up from the sea ...]. Here the sea is tranquil, resplendent with God's Light, translucent: humanity in the state of Grace, redeemed and nourished by the Sacraments of the Church, living before God and for God.

The 'Four Living Beings' represent the Episcopal Office, dignity and authority in the Church. They share the throne with the Deity and with the Lamb. At all times the Living Beings make the final pronouncement, (Authority in Doctrine), put the seal of approval upon worship (Liturgy) and share in the knowledge of Divine Revelation and in God's watchfulness (eyes). They are clearly in the Church on earth, for in Heaven as the 'heavenly dwelling' there is no night.

It is worthy of note that the Four Living Beings represent the Episcopate, the Hierarchy, the collective Bishops united with Christ. Individual bishops are designated by 'Angel', or by 'stars'. (See Chapters 1 & 2).

In this vision, which is continued in the next chapter, the inspired writer has drawn a vivid picture of the constitution and organisation of the Church as it functions today: clearly showing thereby that She was fully organised by the Apostles in all Her essentials at the end of the 1st Century.

Although the devout reader of this chapter is struck by the many references to images met in the writings of the Old Testament, which shows essential continuity and unity of Inspired Writing, the student of these matters will notice some profound differences. E.g. in the Old Testament imagery there is no mention of a 'crystal sea' before the throne of Yahweh. This follows because in that time there was not yet a 'Redeemed Humanity' to be represented. The behavior of the 'Four Living Beings' is sufficiently different in the writings of the old prophets from what it is here to conclude that, in both cases, they represent different realities. Whence the difference?

The answer of course is: *from the Incarnation.* And this brings us back to Our Lady and Her indispensable role in the formation of the Church.

The direct reference to Her in this vision is the mention of 'the door'. A door was opened in heaven … Had the door not been opened St. John would not have seen anything. Once again: 'the door in heaven'. The 'Porta Coeli' in the Litany of Our Lady.

A door was opened in Heaven so that the Second Person of the Blessed Trinity could go through it, and come down to earth. Only one person could assist the Almighty in unlocking that door: Mary, with Her 'Fiat', 'Let it be done'. Only one person, the Virgin Mary, could give to God 'the Key' to unlock the door to the exclusive Sacredness of Her Virginal Womb for the Incarnation to take place, so that it could become 'the Sanctuary of the Most High'. It is only here, then, that we can see and may understand that when Christ, in the previous chapters of the Apocalypse, tells us that He holds '*the Key of David*', i.e. the 'Key to the Redemption', He was once again referring to His Mother. Christ did not say: 'I Am the Key of David', but 'I am the One who holds the Key of David'. He holds absolute and universal dominion, yet He uses chosen instruments ... All the glory and benefits upon which St. John was allowed to gaze through the opened door, are there by the active cooperation of Mary with the saving will of God. They are there by obedience, and by ineffable Love and Trust ...

But there is more to it. The essential unity between the Old Imagery and the New one, this 'borrowing' of the Old to express the New, shows that what took place when God was 'in the Sanctuary of Mary's virginal womb', and only the Old Testament knew that He was there. How the Heavenly Court must have come down on earth to adore the Divine Presence in Mary. How the holy Souls of the Just must have joined in, to form essentially the same tableau depicted here by St. John, so full still of the Old. Through Mary's 'Fiat' the Old and the New are linked, and the fact that both the Old and the New are represented here in this vision (because the 'New' is expressed in images borrowed from the 'Old') shows that

Our Blessed Lady is as present to God in this Vision as are all the other Holy Realities mentioned by St. John. The Church we are shown here in its essential composition and activity, poised to conquer the world and wrest the nations from Satan's grip of iron, *is a Marian Church.* What we contemplate here had already taken place at the Incarnation, where the presence of Our Lady was indispensable. This makes it equally impossible for Her august Person and Her life of virtue to be absent here, in order that the Church we are privileged to see here *can continue to imitate Her, and model Herself on Her* in obedience to the Father's Will ...

Old Testament References in Chapter 4

Dn 2:28. [p. 1425]. (v.1)

See Ch.1, v.1.

Is 6:1. [p. 1151]. (v.2)

In the year of King Uzziah's death I saw the Lord Yahweh seated on a high throne. His train filled the Sanctuary.

1K 22:19. [p. 452]. (v.2)

I have seen Yahweh seated on His throne; all the array of heaven stood in His presence, on His right and on His left.

Ezk 1:26-28. [p. 1363]. (v.2-3)

Above the vault over their heads was something that looked like a sapphire; it was shaped like a throne and high up on this throne was a Being that looked like a man. I saw Him shine like bronze ... [For the remainder see Ch.1, p.24, v.17].

Gn 9:12-17. [p. 24]. (v.3)

God said: "Here is the sign of the Covenant I make between Myself and you, and every living creature with you for all generations. I set My bow in the clouds and it shall be a sign of the Covenant between Me and the earth. When I gather the clouds over the earth and the bow appears in the clouds, I will recall the Covenant between Myself and you and every living creature of every kind. And so the waters shall never again become a flood to destroy all things of flesh. When the bow is in the clouds I shall see it and call to mind the lasting Covenant between God and every living creature of every kind that is found on the earth".

Is 24:5-6. [p. 1178]. (v.3)

The earth is defiled
under its inhabitants' feet.
for they have transgressed the law, violated the precept,
broken the everlasting Covenant.
So a curse consumes the earth [like a Second Flood!]
and its inhabitants suffer the penalty,
that is why the inhabitants of the earth are burnt up
and few men are left.

Is 24:23. [p. 1180]. (v.4)

Yahweh Saboath will be King
on Mount Zion, in Jerusalem,
and His Glory will shine in the presence of His Elders.

Ex 24:10. [p. 108]. (v6)

They saw the God of Israel beneath whose feet there was it seemed,
a sapphire pavement pure as the Heavens themselves.

Ezk 1:5-21.. [p. 1362]. (v.6-8)

Here, at the beginning of the call of Ezekiel, is a description of the vision of the 'Chariot of Yahweh'. The reader is referred to it as it is too long to quote in its entirety.

Ezk 10:14. [p. 1370]. (v.7)

Each Cherub had four faces: the first face was the face of a cherub, the second face the face of a man, the third face the face of a lion, the fourth face the face of an eagle.

Is 6:2. [p. 1151]. (v.8)

Above Him stood Seraphs, each one with six wings …

Ezk 1:18. [p. 1362]. (v.8)

Their rims seemed enormous when I looked at them and all four rims had eyes all the way round.

Ezk 10:12. [p. 1370]. (v.8)

Their bodies, their backs, their hands, their wings and the wheels – the wheels of all four – were covered in eyes all over.

Is 6:3. [p. 1152]. (v.8)

And they cried out to one another in this way,
Holy, Holy, Holy is Yahweh Saboath.
His Glory fills the whole earth. [For confirmation of this by God Himself, see Numbers 14:21].

Dn 4:31. [p. 1433]. (v.9)

'When the time was over, I, Nebuchadnezzar, lifted up my eyes to heaven: my reason returned. And I blessed the Most High, praising and extolling Him who lives forever,
for His Sovereignty is an eternal sovereignty,
His empire lasts from age to age …

Ps 115:3. [p. 900]. (v.11)

Ours is the God whose will is sovereign
in the heavens and on earth

Section 5

The Fifth Chapter in the Book of Revelation
The Adoration of the Lamb

Fr. Kramer's Commentary

In this Chapter the 'Lamb of God' dominates the scene as the centre of the Church. The Sacrificial Lamb as the centre of the Church is of course the Eucharistic Lamb, the Lamb offered up to the Father in the Mass.

The actual dethroning of Satan has already taken place; now the effects of the Redemption have to be taken to all the peoples on earth, and what this holds in store is written in the scroll, sealed with the 7 seals. Since the Lamb has paid the price in His Blood, He alone is found worthy to open the seals and make known God's Decrees as He sees fit.

The remainder of the book of Revelation will be the history of the establishment of the dominion of the Kingdom of God over the world, that is, the story of the progress of the Church. The most important Revelation in this chapter, then, is the Divine Disclosure that this progress is due to the continual renewing in time of the Great Sacrifice of the Mass. It is 'the little Lamb, as it were sacrificed', which is slowly subduing all opposing forces to His sweet dominion. The judgements of God emanate from the Blessed Eucharist as the centre of Creation, and the Blessed Eucharist is at the heart and centre of the Catholic Church.

The Mass is the central reason for the establishment of a Priesthood in the Church. It is through the *Priestly office* first, that the Episcopate also will share in Christ's *Kingship*: exerting dominion over events in time.

It is of no small significance that this is one of the rare occasions in Scripture that the whole of Creation is portrayed as concurring with a decision: the decision that the Mass is the centre and the source of all true progress: the dominion of God on earth. *Daily Communicants in the Catholic Church* are therefore the closest to the only true Power on earth, exerting with Christ the greatest possible influence on the shaping of the destiny of History …

"Next to the Cross of Jesus stood His Mother …"

She had not spared herself in preparing the Lamb for the Paschal Sacrifice. If here in this chapter 'the whole of creation' is seen as giving glory to the Lamb, then, again, we may say: "*Next to the glorified Lamb Jesus stood His Mother …*" She may not yet be visibly present, as, for the moment, it is the will of God *to reveal the Church*; but the gratitude 'of all creation' is there, going out to Her for having prepared 'the little Lamb', which made the Eucharistic Sacrifice possible. In His own good time God will make public the unbreakable bond between His Mother and the Church, laid there 'from the foundation of the world …'

As we have seen, God is beginning to reveal an *indispensable* presence of the Marian Dimension, as indispensable as the Mother is to the Daughter, or the model is to the replica. But, however necessary the Marian presence is, it is still a subordinate existence: as subordinate as the creature is to the Creator. The absolute dominion of the Lamb is unassailable, and must remain so. It is to the everlasting greatness of Mary that, in being the 'Handmaid of the Lord', cooperating in total submission to, and in perfect obedience with the Will of God, 'She became the Mother of God and a cause of our salvation'. (St. Irenaeus, quoted by Vatican II in *Lumen Gentium*). God never forced Her 'Fiat': 'Let it be done'. He never intruded on Her freedom of choice and action. But, having been made perfect, He knew He could depend on Her Obedience and Faith.

And so, even if for the time being the little Lamb is shown alone, His very presence shows the Obedience, Faith and Love of the one who conceived Him and made His existence on earth possible. The Marian Dimension has nothing artificial about it: it is there continuously, waiting to be revealed. It not only surrounds the Church: at one time it completely surrounded and enclosed the Eucharistic Lamb …

This makes it inevitable that truly Eucharistic Catholics are Marian Catholics, and that truly Marian Catholics exert, with the Eucharistic Christ, true dominion over events in time …

Old Testament References in Chapter 5

Is 29:11. [p. 1187]. (v.1-3)

For every vision has become like the words of a sealed book. You give it to someone able to read and say, 'Read that'. He replies, 'I cannot because the book is sealed'. Or else you give the book to someone who cannot read and say, 'Read that'. He replies, 'I cannot read'.

Ezk 2:9-10. [p. 1363]. (v.1)

I looked. A hand was there, stretching out to me and holding a scroll. He unrolled it in front of me; it was written on back and front; on it was written 'lamentations, wailings, moanings'. [See also Zc: 5:2, where a scroll too is connected with punishment].

Dn 12:4. [p. 1446]. (v.1)

But you Daniel must keep these words secret and the book sealed until the time of the End. Many will wander this way and that, and wickedness will go on increasing.

Gn 49:9-10. [p. 74]. (v.5)

Judah is a lion cub … The sceptre shall not pass from Judah until He comes to whom it belongs.

Is 11:1. [p. 1160]. (v.5)

A shoot springs from the stock of Jesse, A scion thrusts from his roots …

Is 11:10. [p. 1161]. (v.5)

That day, the root of Jesse shall stand as a signal to the peoples …

Zc 4:10. [p. 1532]. (v.6)

He then gave me this answer: 'These seven are the eyes of Yahweh; they cover the whole world'.

Is 61:6. [p. 1240]. (v.10)

"… but you, you will be named 'Priests of Yahweh', they will call you 'ministers of our God' …"

Ex 19:6. [p. 101]. (v.10)

"… I will count you a kingdom of Priests, a consecrated nation".
[See also this same quote in Section I.]

Dn 7:10. [p. 1437]. (v.11)

A thousand thousand waited on Him,
ten thousand times ten thousand stood before Him.

Dn 2:20. [p. 1424]. (v.12)

"May the Name of God
be blessed for ever and ever,
since Wisdom and Power are His alone …"

Ps 150:6. [p. 930]. (v.13)

Let everything that breathes praise Yahweh.

Section 6

The Sixth Chapter in the Book of Revelation
The Breaking of the First Six Seals

Fr. Kramer's Commentary

It is essential to remember that what is being written in the Apocalypse are *the Judgements of God* from the centre of His Church *within the history of His Church.* As St. Peter had already declared in the Name of God, and with the Authority of God: "For it is time that judgement should begin at the House of God". (1 Peter 4:17). If, then, on the opening of the First Seal by the Lamb, a rider on a white horse appears, then this relates to an historical happening, seen as a Judgement of God, in relation to His Church. This, for several reasons, rules out Christ as the rider as well as the 'victorious Gospel'. For one, Christ is not 'under the judgement of God'. Christ cannot, as the Sacrificial Lamb, open the seals and then be called out by some delegated authority as a warrior. The 'bow' inflicts wounds but does not destroy. The sword is the symbol of total destruction, which, in relation to Christ, when used against the wicked, is His Word, His command. (The sword comes out of His Mouth). To represent Christ as a common warrior with a bow killing whom He can hit, is an affront to His Divine Majesty. If the rider is on a par with the other horsemen, he is a scourge; and nowhere in Scripture is Christ, or His saving Gospel, depicted as a scourge. If the Gospel were a war-like conqueror it would be a death-dealing rather than a joyous message. Besides, Scripture could then be quoted against the Gospel for in Zacharias 9:10 it is written, 'the bow of the warrior shall be broken'.

For these considerations, then, it is fitting to see in the *white* horse and the *laurel wreath* what was a familiar sight in those days: a victorious Roman general, *as a symbol of the victorious Roman armies, inimical to the Church.* Under God's Judgement, then, the Roman Empire would be victorious for a while, would inflict wounds on the Church in persecutions; but would not destroy Her, and would also be an instrument in His Hands for paving the way for the future spread of the Gospel. Such considerations would give consolation to His beloved Church, and would sustain Her in Her hour of trial and tribulation.

With the same depth of understanding Fr. Kramer then goes through the other 'Five Seals'.

On opening the Second Seal a Red Horse appears symbolizing sacrifice and bloodshed, caused by revolutions and uprisings; the most famous of that time was the Jewish Rebellion. The 'great sword' symbolizes some total destruction. Emperor Hadrian, in a war that lasted five years, 131 – 135, devastated the whole of the Palestinian countryside, putting an end to the Jewish national existence. Fifty cities, a thousand villages and four hundred and eighty synagogues were wiped out. The inhabitants were either massacred or sold into slavery. The ruin of the nation was complete and final. The Christian population did not take part in the uprising and was not molested. The extinction of the Jewish nation was of vast importance to the Church.

Here we have a splendid example we can use to briefly show the reader how Fr. Kramer went to work in his commentary on the Apocalypse and why, after twenty five years (he first published it in 1955) it still has so much with which to recommend itself.

Fr. Kramer follows strictly the rules laid down by St. John and the Holy Spirit in the Book of Revelation itself:

(i) He looks for an historical event which is past for us, but future for St. John. In Apoc. 4:1 the latter was told by Divine authority that he was going to be shown things *which must befall hereafter*, i.e. historical events.

(ii) The event must be viewed from the point of view of God, i.e. *as a Judgement of God*. In Apoc. 4:2 God is seen sitting on His throne, His seat of Judgement.

(iii) The event must be intimately related to the Church. In Apoc. 4:2 the throne from which the Judgements of God are made is seen in the centre of the Church; it is not His throne in Heaven as such. In 1 Peter 4:17 we get confirmation of this from a Pope who also speaks with God's Authority.

(iv) The historical event which Fr. Kramer 'selects' as an explanation of the imagery used by St. John, must be in line with the image used, must 'fit' it, and the explanation he gives to the image in order that it may fit his chosen event, must be consistent with its use elsewhere in Sacred Scripture. It is especially in this area that Fr. Kramer's use of the Old Testament is invaluable, and it is for that reason that I have gone to the trouble of printing those quotes after each chapter for easy reference.

If we add to this that we must always remember that a logical or plausible 'immediate fulfillment' of a prophecy, however obvious it may look to us, does not exhaust it and does not prevent it from having another, additional, actualisation later on, then it will do us no harm getting acquainted with Fr. Kramer's descriptions and conclusions. And, because of the safeguards used, we would not go far wrong even if we went along with them.

The opening of the Third Seal reveals the existence of famine during a protracted war. This revelation is of interest, since it is the Church which takes a hand in the relief of the effects by deciding the prices. This 'price-fixing' prevented 'black-marketeering' and made sure that there was enough to go round at a price which a frugal, hardworking father of a family could afford. Also, because of God's concern for the young Christian communities, more durable crops were not affected. Although war and famine are scourges permitted by God for sin, which at the same time also show His Mercy, for they give time for repentance, they are mitigated for His faithful servants.

The breaking of the Fourth Seal reveals depopulation of a fourth part of the earth through death caused by pestilence, accompanied by the other three great scourges often enumerated bracketed together by the old prophets. In the old days mainly directed at the Jews for their apostasy, they nearly always are extended to include their oppressors. So here we see God's Judgement starting to work on the breaking up of the Roman Empire as a world power because of the persecutions of the Church, to make room for the Church for the good of mankind. For the imagery used here refers to the invasions of the Barbarians, which always meant new diseases, wars, famine, bloodshed.

When the Divine Lamb opened the Fifth Seal a different Judgement of God in relation to His Beloved Church became manifest. The Martyrs' cry of anguish is but an audible utterance of what, down the ages in times of great distress, must have been prayed silently over and over again by all who are consumed with hunger and thirst for the Justice of God: 'How long, O Lord …?' The 'altar' is the foot of the Cross, and we are reminded of the unbelievable insults and mockery, thrown up at our dying Saviour in the Face of God.

By allowing the cry to be heard, God makes known that He has supreme reasons for the delay, and that *rest* is the reward for confidence in His Absolute Perfection. The 'rest' St. John talks about here is not the eternal rest after death. We are not dealing with the dead: we are constantly dealing with the 'living': the Church on earth. The rest here is the peace we get, even under the most adverse conditions, as the result of utter abandonment to God's will; from total trust in His Absolute Holiness.

The opening of the Sixth Seal causes the powers of Heaven to be moved. 'Heaven', here again, is the Church. We are dealing then with a spiritual commotion or disturbance, a religious revolution of colossal magnitude. This is corroborated by the darkening of the sun and moon, and the falling of the stars. We are reminded of Christ's words to His Apostles: "You are the Light of the world". The Sun symbolizes the greatest Light in the Church, *the Divinity of Christ*, which gives absolute force to Her teaching authority. The Moon represents here the changeable elements in the Church, which derive their right from Her Divine teaching authority (the Moon receives her light from the Sun). The darkening Sun shows growing unbelief in the Divinity of Christ, and the darkening of the moon indicates disobedience. Heresies in the Church (don't we know it!) have always spawned hatred, distrust, fraud, intrigues, envies, pride, violence, murders, immorality and even wars.

The 'falling of numerous stars from heaven' represents individual bishops and priests defecting from the Supernatural state of Grace through their heresies, with the result that they find themselves outside the Church (back on earth). All of this unmistakably points to the *Arian heresy*, as the principal suspect for this 'Judgement of God', and the main cause of damage done to the Church, so graphically described here. The Arian heresy started in AD 318, immediately after the overthrow of Paganism as an opposing force to the Church, and must be considered as the last and most deadly attempt of paganism to reassert itself. After AD 359, the Council of Rimini, the Arians were everywhere so triumphant, that, from the viewpoint of the laity, the Church must have appeared 'as a volume rolled up'. The punishment was swift and came before the Faith was altogether too reduced to be capable of converting the invading hordes of Barbarians. If these, in turn, clung to Arianism, they fell under the sway of the Saracens. The Byzantine empire had become heir to the roman empire but became the principal promoter of heresy, for which it lost the whole Western part of the empire, including Africa. 'All the islands and mountains were removed from their places…'.

It is in times of heresy preaching, more than at any other time, that the hatred of the Devil and his seed, the heretics, for the Woman, meets with the power of the Marian Dimension within the Church, the Woman's seed. In a magnificent effort, a reprint of which is overdue, a great Catholic author has shown in 1851, i.e. before the Dogma of the Immaculate Conception and in defense of that Dogma, *that all heresies tend to Manicheism, and consequently to hatred of 'the Immunity'*. [Fr. John Brande Morris, MA, in his two-volumed: *Jesus the Son of Mary, or The Doctrine of the Catholic Church upon the Incarnation of God the Son, considered in its bearing upon the Reverence shewn by Catholics to his Blessed Mother*.]

To prove his point, this learned Priest, towards the end of his book, goes through the internal composition of every known heresy. What Catholic in our days has not suffered from the hatred shown by modernism towards the Mother of God … The silent hostility by which She is surrounded in those quarters! … The lip service modernist periodicals and catechetical hand-outs pay grudgingly to Her in order to remain accepted as 'catholic'! Much more about that later.

If we accept Fr. Kramer's chronology of the Sixth chapter of the Apocalypse as being correct, then this chapter spans the period of greatest theological debate in the Church; in which most of the questions concerning Christ and the Church were settled. Nearly all of the most illustrious Doctors and Fathers of the Church lived in that period; which also included a number of the Great Councils of the Church: notably the Council of Nicaea, AD 325, which condemned Arianism; and the Council of Ephesus, AD 431, which condemned Nestorianism and Pelagianism, and defined the Dogma of the Divine Maternity of Mary.

All of the great names of the day, too many to even enumerate here, concerned themselves with defining the Church's teaching on Our Lady; and there can be little doubt that, next to the Blessed Eucharist, it was love for the Mother of God which sustained the laity through the terrible time of the Arian heresy, which, according to the great Cardinal Newman, lasted for more than sixty years …

A most fortuitous foundation for Mariology was laid by St. Ireneus in assigning to Mary the role of 'The New Eve', cooperating with 'The New Adam' (St. Paul), to undo what had been tied-up by the 'Proto-Parents' lapse from Grace. St. Ireneus was a disciple of St. Polycarp who in turn was a disciple of St. John. There can be no doubt the New Adam – New Eve parallel has Apostolic origin.

Vatican II has completely restored the force of St Ireneus' approach, and not only drew our attention to it, but used this first century foundation for the consolidation and elaboration of the Mariology of the twentieth century. The consoling truth of the *Marian Dimension* has now been completely vindicated by the highest teaching authority in the Church. At a time when 'the sum total of all heresies' (Pope St. Pius X), Modernism, is again eating the heart out of the Catholic Church, our Holy Mother the Catholic Church does not hesitate to send us right back to the First Prophecy in Paradise: where the foundations of our deliverance were laid …

Why is this so important? In the ecumenical climate of today, many Protestant Christians are taking a fresh look at Catholic doctrine. For those Christians it is necessary to learn that the love and devotion for Our Blessed Lady by Catholics is not only based on Her privileges, but even more so on what She has done and suffered for our sake. The 'New Eve' role of Our Lady is not only Biblical, is not only Apostolic, does not only take our minds back to Genesis: it is humanely appealing. It demands a response. It makes the Marian Dimension so logical, so plausible, so attractive and inviting. So easy to accept … The 'New Eve': mother of all the Living. Mother of all those born to Eternal Life. Nowhere in the whole Bible was Our Lady ever in the way of God, in the way of Christ. On the contrary. As 'Eve' was in Adam's way, tying his hands, so to speak, hampering his free decision, so the 'New Eve' gave God free reign. She was in everything the exact opposite of Her counter-part in Genesis. And this not for some other human being, but for the Son of God. It is unnatural, artificial and contrived to see in that anything other than what it really is: *the greatest possible Holiness and Virtue in a woman …*

Old Testament References in Chapter 6

Jr 15:2-4. [p. 1277] (v.1f)

[1. Yahweh said to me, 'Even if Moses and Samuel were standing in My presence I could not warm to these people. Drive them out of My sight; away with them.']. 'and if they ask you, "Where shall we go?", tell them this, "Yahweh says this:

Those for the plague, to the plague;
those for the sword, to the sword;
those for famine, to famine;
those for captivity, into captivity!"

Four kinds of doom I consign them to: the sword to kill, the dogs to drag away, the birds of heaven and the beasts of earth to devour and destroy. I will make them an object of horror to all the kingdoms of earth ...'

Ezk 5:17. [p. 1366]. (v.1f)

"Against you I mean to send famine and wild animals, to rob you of your children; plague and bloodshed shall visit you. I will summon the sword against you. I, Yahweh, have spoken".

Ezk 14:13-21. [p. 1374]. (v.1f)

"Son of man, if a country were to sin against Me by faithlessness, and if I were to stretch out My hand against it and destroy its stock of bread and send famine to it to kill its men and beasts, and if in that country there were these three men, Noah, Daniel and Job, these men would have their lives spared because of their integrity – it is the Lord Yahweh who speaks. Were I to unleash wild animals on that country to rob it of its children and reduce it to such a desert that no one would dare to cross it because of the animals, and if these three men were in that country, then, as I live, - it is the Lord Yahweh who speaks – they would not be able to save either son or daughter; they alone would be saved, and the country would become a desert. If I were to bring the sword into that country …"

Zc 1:8-10. [p. 1530]. (v.2-8)

"I saw a vision during the night. It was this: a man riding a red horse among the deep rooted myrtles; behind him were horses, red and sorrel and black and white. I said: 'What are these my lord?' And the Angel who was talking to me said: 'I will explain to you what they are'. The man standing among the myrtles answered, 'They are those whom Yahweh has sent to patrol throughout the world'."

Zc 6:1-3. [p. 1534]. (v.2-8)

Again I raised my eyes, and this is what I saw: four chariots coming out between the two mountains, and the mountains were mountains of bronze. The first chariot had red horses, the second had black horses, the third chariot had white horses, and the fourth chariot had piebald horses. I asked the Angel who was talking to me, I said, 'What is the meaning of these my lord?' The Angel answered, 'These are going out to the four winds of heaven after standing before the Lord of the whole world'.

Ezk 21:14-16. [p. 1384]. (v.4

"Son of man, prophesy. Say, 'The Lord says this'. Say:
'The sword, the sword, sharpened and polished.
Sharpened for slaughter, polished to flash like lightning.

Polished only to be wielded, sharpened and polished to fit the slaughterer's hand ..."

Lv 26:26. [p. 165]. (v.6)

I will take away from you your bread, which is your staff, and one oven shall suffice for ten women to bake your bread; they shall dole this bread out by weight, and you shall eat and not be filled.

Ezk 4:16f [p. 1365]. (v.6)

He then said, "Son of man, I mean to destroy the stock of bread in Jerusalem; in their distress they will eat bread strictly weighed; in terror they will drink water grudgingly measured, since bread and water will be scarce; they will pine away and waste away as a result of their sins".

Ezk 14:21. [p. 1374]. (v.8)

The Lord Yahweh says this: "Now if I do send My four dreadful scourges against Jerusalem – sword, famine, wild animals and plague – to cut off its men and beasts and if any survivors are left there to contrive the escape of son and daughter, they will come for you to see their conduct and actions and so be comforted in spite of the scourges ..."

Dt 32:43. [p. 259]. (v.10)

"Heavens rejoice with Him, let the sons of God pay Him homage!

Nations, rejoice with his people, let God's envoys tell of His power!

For He will avenge the blood of His servants, He will give his foes as good again!

He will repay those who hate Him, and purify the land of His people!"

[The whole *Song of Moses* is worth reading in this context].

Jb 16:18+ [p.746]. (v.10)

Cover not my blood, O earth,
afford my cry no place to rest.
Henceforth I have a witness in heaven,
my Defender is there in the height.

Jb 24:12. [p. 755]. (v.10-11)

From the towns come the groans of the dying,
and the gasp of wounded men crying for help.
Yet God remains deaf to their appeal.

Zc 1:12-13. [p. 1530]. (v.10)

The Angel of Yahweh then spoke and said,

"Yahweh Saboath, how long will You wait before taking pity on Jerusalem and the cities of Judah, on which You have inflicted your anger for the past seventy years? ..."

"I feel most jealous love for Jerusalem and Zion, but very bitter anger against the proud nations. They have overstepped all limits".

Dn 8:13,14. [p. 1439]. (v.10)

I heard a holy one speaking, and another who said to the speaker, "How long is this vision to be – of Perpetual Sacrifice, disastrous iniquity, of sanctuary and army trampled underfoot?" The first replied, "Until two thousand three hundred evenings and mornings have gone by: then the sanctuary shall have its rights restored".

Jl 3:4. [p. 1474]. (v. 12,17)

The sun will be turned into darkness,
and the moon into blood,
before the Day of Yahweh dawns,
the great and terrible day.

Is 34:4. [p. 1195]. (v. 14)

The heavens are rolled up like a scroll
and their armies all drop like leaves …

Is 2:10,18,19. [p. 1145-6]. (v. 15-17)

Get among the rocks, hide in the dust,
at the sight of the terror of Yahweh.
Go into the hollows of the rocks,
into the caverns of the earth,
at the sight of the terror of Yahweh,
at the brilliance of His Majesty,
when He arises to make the earth quake.

Ho 10:8. [p. 1463]. (v. 16)

Then they will say to the mountains, 'Cover us!'
and to the hills, 'Fall on us!'

Jl 2:11. [p. 1472]. (v. 17)

As they come on, the earth quakes,
the skies tremble, sun and moon grow dark,
the stars lose their brilliance.
Yahweh makes His voice heard at the head of His army …
For great is the Day of Yahweh: who can face it?

Section 7

The Seventh Chapter in the Book of Revelation
The Fruits of the Early Victory of the Church

Fr. Kramer's Commentary

The First Six Seals narrated the destruction of the Old Order in the world. The Little Lamb, the Eucharistic King, accomplished this. Judaism and Paganism were overthrown by His direction of world affairs.

But Satan was not fully vanquished. Hardly had the Church triumphed over the two Great Enemies, when Satan, working now within the Church, misled many bishops and priests into the heresies of Arianism, Monophysitism, Nestorianism and other religious vagaries.

But the Lamb was not to be defeated. He summoned the Barbarians to wipe out the sectaries and then called these instruments of His Providence into the fold. And before the Holy Seer narrates to us what next 'must befall hereafter' (Apoc.4:1), in describing to us world events in relation to the Church when the Lamb opens the 7th Seal (in Chapter 8), our attention is first directed to the *Blessings of the Gospel*, described in two visions in the present chapter, which, under the same Divine Influence of the Eucharistic Lamb, are intended for the benefit of all men.

The first of these two visions is the announcement of the long-awaited judgement of God against all unbelievers, delayed only until the Church has won sufficient influence, so that through Her all who will avail themselves of Her blessings, may do so, since these Judgements are primarily intended to destroy sin, not the sinner.

The second vision shows the Church in the exercise of Her hard-won influence, taking over the affairs of the nations with great strength and wisdom, radiating the divine light of Truth through the whole world. This Chapter 7 must not be seen as an interlude between two 'seals', but as something that became manifest sometime after the overthrow of the Roman Empire, and must stay with the believing readers for their consolation, until its full and world-wide realisation *after the crushing of Antichrist* has been accomplished, of which the overthrow of the Roman Empire is only an example, a type and pre-figuration. This blessing must be seen as an ideal state, something that, by God's Will, was partially realised once, to let us see what it will be on a world-wide scale later on, in Chapter XXI.

The last chapter ended with the words, 'who shall be able to stand?' [Jl 2:11]. The present chapter answers that question with the response, 'those whom the Lamb shall rule'.

'Winds' represent 'revolutions in human society' [Dn 8:2] or 'invading armies, charioteers' [Zc 6:5]. Here they are forecast to bring the judgements of God, not to a fourth of the earth, but over the whole earth. They are universal. In the next chapter the four winds come on the scene in new forms. So we must benefit from the meaning given to these events here. They 'blow' for the benefit of the Church, as a Judgement of God. 'Winds' also blow chaff out of the Church: apostates and heretics unwilling to leave the visible confines of the Church in order to better exert their 'power' over

Her, trying to force Her to walk ways according to their modernistic ideas. A vain hope …

The 'earth', 'sea' and 'trees' are mentioned to show the universal character of God's visitation when it comes. The ruin and devastation of the revolution will strike first of all 'the earthlings': all those who have set their hopes and desires on things terrestrial instead of spiritual; the results will be universal, and will affect all humanity: the 'sea' as well as governments, civil and military leaders: the 'trees'.

The Judgements of God will not come to pass until such time that the Church has made full use of the delay for the benefit of the elect, taken from the Jews as well as the Gentiles.

Here is one place in the apocalypse where the immediate meaning of the narrative has a strong eschatological meaning as well.

- The *Roman Persecutions are now officially over*, but these were only a preview of worse to come: *the Persecutions under Antichrist.*
- The *gratitude* of the Church on earth in these earlier times narrated here, is clearly an image of the *immense gratitude* of the Church on earth after Antichrist, when the whole world will be placed under the sweet dominion of the Eucharistic Lamb.
- The *partial conversion of the Jews* at the time of Julian the Apostate's effort to rebuild the temple roundabout the time of this chapter, is only a foreshadowing of the tremendous glory to the Church when the remnant of Israel will enter Her after Antichrist.

- The '*seal of the Living God*' contrasts sharply with '*the mark of the beast*' at the time of Antichrist.
- And finally, the glory of the *Marian Dimension* of the Church of those earlier times will break out into full bloom, and will carry the greatest fruits, before and during the confrontation of the Church with the full force of Antichrist.

In having alone, out of all creation, been found worthy to break the 7 seals of the Church's future, and the future of all humanity in relation to its new centre: the Catholic Church, the Lamb of God was not only found worthy to *know* this future, or been given power to *reveal it* to whom He pleases: He was given the complete authority *to direct that future from His Eucharistic Throne in the Sanctuary of His Church.*

This must be one of the most powerful and consoling Revelations to come from the Book of Revelation.

The whole history of the Human Race consists of an almost endless procession and succession of freely willed human acts, yet none of them escape the more superior free Will of God, Who directs everyone of them towards the greater good of His Elect. After His Sacrificial Death on the Cross the Lamb of God has the complete authority to direct world affairs to the greater good and glory of His Church. This is a Divine Prerogative alone. Only God can do this, and the Lamb of God is Divine.

One of those myriads of freely performed human acts permitted Him entry into this world. Permitted Him entrance into the Virginal Womb of His Most Blessed Mother; and the Lamb of God so loved this Sanctuary where He was completely at home, surrounded only by good without so much as the shadow of an imperfection, that He formed a Church 'in the image and likeness of His Mother', so that He could stay in that Sanctuary knowing that all who loved him would mould themselves on Her in order to please Him and to make him feel at home. And from the Eucharistic Throne '*within the Sanctuary of His Church*', the Lamb of god would direct world affairs to the greater glory of His Church, and would direct his Church in the image and likeness of His Mother to the greater glory of God, as well as of His Blessed Mother.

No wonder, then, that in this present chapter of the apocalypse, where we are so vividly reminded of the future by various aspects of the narrative, we are once again brought into the sacred presence of the *Sanctuary* of the Eucharistic Lamb, to remind us of the first Sanctuary where He dwelt; to remind us of the continued presence of that first Sanctuary in His Church in the Marian Dimension; to remind us that the praise and gratitude for the Redemption going out from the Sanctuary of His Church first went up from that original Sanctuary, the Proto-type of the present one; and finally to bring home to us that 'recourse to His Blessed Mother' in all the events of life, but especially in persecutions, is automatically 'entering into His presence', for not only is He found there, but She will lead anyone who comes to Her to His Eucharistic throne. *For it is the task of any Sanctuary to draw attention to the presence of the One who dwells in it.*

To reinforce the truth, that both the Divine author, as well as His chosen instrument, St. John, are referring here to an earthly situation, a period of the Church in time, words and phrases have been chosen here, which preclude direct reference to the 'bliss of heaven', although of course any happy and blessed state in the Church on earth is a natural uplifter towards our heavenly existence.

i. '... day and night in His Sanctuary'. There is no night in Heaven.
ii. 'They have washed their robes and made them white in the Blood of the Lamb'. They did not wash them in their own blood by being martyred. They were Eucharistic people, who treasured sanctifying Grace nourished by frequent Communion: the Blood of the Eucharistic Lamb.
iii. The references to the horrors of persecutions in which their relatives and friends were killed, are being taken away from them. It is now a time for being led by the Lamb to spread the fruits of the Gospel, and to enjoy the many treasures of the Church: the fountains of living water.
iv. The last sentence in this chapter: '*and God shall wipe away every tear from their eyes*', is there not only for the above reasons: Divine consolation here on earth after persecutions, but also to make sure that its exact repeat in Ch. 21:4 will again be understood in a still temporal meaning and setting, when these later faithful too will have emerged 'from the great tribulation' of Antichrist, in which countless fellow Christians will have been slain. These later survivors will also be granted a period of great freedom and bliss for the Church, of which the description in this chapter, although historical in its own setting, is nevertheless also a preview and consolation.

Old Testament References in Chapter 7

Ezk 7:2. [p. 1367]. (v.1)

The Lord Yahweh says this to the land of Israel: "Finished! The end is coming for the four quarters of the land. Now all is over with you. I mean to unleash My anger on you, and judge you as your conduct deserves and force you to answer for all your filthy practices ..."

Jr 49:36. [p. 1329]. (v.1)

I will bring four winds down on Elam from the four corners of the sky, and I will scatter the Elamites to the winds.

Zc 6:5. [p. 1534]. (v.1)

The Angel answered, "These are going out to the four winds of heaven after standing before the Lord of the whole world ..."

Is 44:5+ [p. 1212]. (v.3)

One man will say, "I belong to Yahweh",
another will call himself by Jacob's name.
On his hand another will write "Yahweh',
and be surnamed "Israel".

Ezk 9:4. [p. 1369]. (v.2-3)

"Go all through the city, all through Jerusalem, and mark a cross on the foreheads of all who deplore and disapprove of all the filth practiced in it".

Ex 9:4. [p. 90]. (v.4)

The story of the Passover.

"When I see the blood I will pass over you and you shall escape the destroying plague when I strike the land of Egypt".

Gn 15:5. [p. 30]. (v.9)

Then taking him outside, He said, "Look up to heaven and count the stars if you can. Such will be your descendants" He told him. Abram put his faith in Yahweh who counted this as making him justified.

Dn 3:4. [p. 1426]. (v.9)

The herald then made this proclamation: "Men of all peoples, nations, languages! This is required of you: the moment you hear the sound, you must prostrate yourselves and worship the golden statue erected by king Nebuchadnezzar ..."

Is 4:5-6. [p. 1148]. (v.15-16)

[4. When the Lord has washed away the filth of the daughter of Zion and cleansed Jerusalem of the blood, shed in her with the blast of judgement and the blast of destruction,]

5: Yahweh will come out and rest
on the whole stretch of Mount Zion
and on those who are gathered there,
a cloud by day, and smoke,
and by night the brightness of a flaring fire.
For, over all, the Glory of Yahweh
will be a canopy and a tent
to give shade by day from the heat,
refuge and shelter from the storm and rain.

Is 25:4. [p. 1180]. (v.15-16)

"... for you are a refuge for the poor,
a refuge for the needy in distress,
a shelter from the storm,
a shade from the heat ..."

Is 49:10. [p. 1222]. (v.16)

They will never hunger or thirst,
scorching wind and sun shall never plague them;
for He who pities them will lead them
and guide them to springs of water.

Is 25:8. [p. 1180] (v.17)

The Lord Yahweh will wipe away
the tears from every cheek;
He will take away His people's shame everywhere on earth,
For Yahweh has said so.

Chapter Five

From St. Anthony of Egypt to Luther's Revolt
From the Reformation to the Nineteenth Century
Chapters Eight, Nine and Ten of the Apocalypse

As stated before, the first Six Seals narrated the destruction of the Old World Order. The Little Lamb, the Eucharistic King, accomplished this.

And before the Inspired Seer St. John can describe the further development of the world, of the Church, and of both good and evil, he is taken back a bit in time and shown another phase of the conflict: *the preparedness of the Church to survive the Fall of the Roman Empire and to meet the Barbarians.* The great love of Christ does not only encompass His Church, but extends to all those who, in time, will come in contact with Her, will submit to Her sweet yoke and will benefit from Her unique existence. He had designed his church in such a way, that all Her hidden benefits and potentialities would well up from the 'fountains of Eternal Life' within Her, which would bring forth the required graces at the appropriate time. We are about to witness the ripening of one of those Divine Fruits, grown from the innermost secrets of Her Virginal fertility, a fruit for which the outside world was both hungry and ready.

So, in the next chapter of the Apocalypse, Chapter 8, the Seventh Seal reveals the New order that Christ planted in the world through His church, and its growth up to the savage invasion of the Barbarians (the First Trumpet), called by God to finish off the Old order and to pave the way for the New, the establishment of which was announced by the opening of the Seventh Seal.

Section 8

The Eighth Chapter in the Book of Revelation
The Opening of the Seventh Seal
The First Four Trumpets

Fr. Kramer's Commentary

'Half an hour's silence in the Church.' The silence of contemplation, meditation, adoration: an apt beginning of what is to come. It calls to mind the interval in the previous chapter, before the 'Four Winds' are allowed to blow.

Seven angels are standing in the presence of God. It recalls Tobias, 12:15, where the Archangel *Raphael* reveals he is one of those seven. Or they could be great Saints God shall call up at critical times in the history of His Church to warn the people and defend Her.

In the Old Testament *the altar of incense* was overlaid with pure gold. It stood next to the Ark of the Covenant, and was separated from the Holy of Holiest by only a simple curtain [Ex 30:1-9]. 'An everlasting incense' (the fire on this altar as that on the altar of holocausts was never to be extinguished) was to be burned upon it mornings and evenings. In the Psalms, prayer was imagined to ascend to God like incense. In Hebr. 9:1-10 St. Paul claims for the golden altar of incense a close association with the presence of God. In the Holy of Holiest was the throne of God, and the golden altar of incense was nearest to it. [Ex 40:5].

The 'golden altar' in St. John's vision, then, typifies a grand institution in the Church, *the Religious Orders*, and especially *the Contemplative Life*, the life of prayer, self-denial and self-sacrifice, 'a fire never to be extinguished ...'. Nothing in the history of the Church has been of greater importance in shaping Her destiny and spreading Her influence than the Religious Orders. They appeared in this century between the end of the persecutions and the beginning of the barbarian invasions. The 'father of monastic life', St. Anthony, died in 356. By 372 there were 100,000 monks in Egypt. St Athanasius translated the monastic life to the West in 340. By the end of the 4th century it had spread throughout the West and the East.

The thunder accompanying the casting of the golden censer on the earth symbolizes the preaching of God's Word to the nations still in barbarism, closely followed by the Gifts of the Holy Ghost, lightnings. The 'voices' symbolize *the Oral Tradition* in the Church, by which the Gospel and the Church's teachings were being spread around and handed on after the initial preaching by the Monks. The earthquake rumbles forth the overthrow of the social, religious and political institutions of paganism, recalling the earthquake in Ch. 6 which revealed the abolition of the Roman state religion.

The greatest example of a life ever lived in total absorption in Jesus Christ, is the Life of His Holy Mother. And here we see one of the most wonderful offshoots of the *Marian Dimension*: the Religious Life, being founded as a permanent institution in the Bride of the Lamb of God, the Catholic Church. St. Methodius says of the 'golden altar':

> "Moreover, it has been handed down that the unbloody altar of God signifies the assembly of the chaste: thus *virginity* appears to be something precious, something great and glorious." (Banquet of the Ten Virgins, VI).

This links the whole of the monastic life once again to the 'golden altar of the Apocalypse', and through it to the Life of virginity of both Christ and His Blessed Mother. The annals of the Religious Life are overflowing with testimonies of the singular devotion to the Mother of God the holy men and women practised in the monastic life; and of their continuous recourse to Our Lady, to help them imitate Her in Her life of poverty, chastity, obedience to God's Will, Her life of prayer and contemplation, Her life of continuous service to the Church.

We have seen that the extension of the Marian Dimension from the Old Testament into the New is God's Will, and is carried on by Christ out of reverence for His Father's Will. It is not hard to see here one of the reasons that could have prompted God: the inspiration of Mary's life helped the establishment of the Religious Life as a permanent, clear, visible and most powerful mark of the true Church founded by His Son.

Fr. Kramer again:

To finish off this important chapter of the Apocalypse, we will briefly summarize here how Fr. Kramer sees the succession and development of historical events, portrayed by the sounding of the first of the four trumpets.

In the Old Testament the imagery of 'trumpets' was invariably used by the Prophets to warn the Jews of approaching *armies and enemies* as punishments from God for their sins. The Prophets even referred to themselves as 'trumpets of God': Jr: 6:17. See also Osee 8:1 and Joel 2:1. The 'trumpets' then herald the 'winds' spoken of in the preceding chapter.

The first trumpet blast is followed by hail and fire, mingled with blood. From Ezk 13:11 we may get a better understanding of what is being alluded to here. There, 'hail' is an instrument of God's Judgement. It is not real hail, but *hostile, marauding, pillaging, plundering armies*. In Ezekiel they come as a punishment for *heresy* and its aftermath: immorality. This trumpet blast accurately describes, then, the invasion of the Roman Empire by the hordes of barbarians which swarmed all over it.

All Christian historians agree that the Barbarians had a mission from God. They came to crush out the last vestiges of paganism in the Roman Empire, as well as the proliferation of Arianism and Nestorianism amongst the Christians. In St. Augustine's time North Africa counted 600 bishoprics. But Africa was over grown with heresy. The Vandals conquered it in 450, and, after adopting Arianism themselves, persecuted the Christians almost to extinction.

What happened to the Vandals?. The second trumpet blast will tell us.

On the sound of the Second Trumpet St. John saw an enormous mass, a 'burning mountain', being hurled into the 'sea'. Fr. Kramer is most convincing, down to the finest detail, in ascribing to this 'image' the event of *the advent of Mohammedanism* in the history of Christianity.

The scourge announced by the Third Trumpet comes down from 'heaven': from the Church itself. It is a 'great star', which is not extinguished in its fall. A metropolitan bishop? Not falling into formal heresy, but into schism? The name 'Wormwood' alludes to this. Neither the name nor the image itself refer directly to the fact of formal heresy, killing Supernatural Life almost instantly; but the historical event which it represents made everything bitter, killing eventually through sickness. The obvious candidate pointed at is the Great Greek Schism, from A.D. 857 onwards, which through its disobedience perverted the sources of spiritual life. It was inevitably finalised in 1054.

At the sound of the Fourth Angel's Trumpet the lights of heaven are dimmed. They stay in place, unlike the previous star, but are a dire calamity in the Church that followed the Greek Schism. The episode referred to here, Fr. Kramer identifies for us as the Great Western 'Schism': a time of Popes and anti-popes, of worldliness in the Church dignitaries, and general laxity amongst the Christians with the inevitable result of heresy preaching in many places.

The Four Scourges announced by the first four trumpets afflicted the earth, the sea, the rivers and fountains of water, and the sun, moon and stars. All phases of life were thus drawn into common misery. They are the 'four winds' of the previous chapter. They will eventually call down on the world the 'woes' of the three remaining trumpets.

But the Eucharistic Presence, and its Handmaid the Marian Dimension, remained within the Church, untouched and unaffected: guiding the Barque of St. Peter on its appointed course through its appointed leaders, the Popes.

And the Great Eagle announcing the three 'woes'? Fr. Kramer identifies him as St. Vincent Ferrer: the great Dominican preacher and missionary of the 15th Century. He seems to be on solid ground here; for this Saint, on declaring himself to be 'the Angel of the Judgement' referred to by St. John in the apocalypse, raised a dead woman back to life to ask her to testify to the truth of his claim, which she did, whereupon he allowed her to go back to sleep again in death.

Old Testament References in Chapter 8

Hab 2:20. [p. 1517]. (v.1)

But Yahweh is in his Holy temple:
Let the whole earth be silent before him.

Zp 1:7. [p. 1520]. (v.1)

Silence before the Lord Yahweh!
For the Day of Yahweh is near.

Zc 2:17. [p. 1532]. (v.1)

Let all mankind be silent before Yahweh!
For He is awakening and is coming from His Holy Dwelling.

Tb 12:15. [p. 617]. (v.2)

"I am Raphael, one of the seven Angels who stand ever ready to enter the presence of the glory of the Lord".

Tb 12:12. [p. 617]. (v.3-4)

"So you must know that when you and Sarah were at prayer, it was I who offered your supplications before the glory of the Lord and who read them".

Ps 141:2. [p. 923]. (v.3-4)

My prayers rise like incense,
my hands like the evening offering.

Lv 16:12. [p. 151]. (v.5)

Then he (Aaron) is to fill a censer with live coals from the altar that stands before Yahweh.

Ezk 10:2. [p. 1369]. (v.5

He then said to the man in white, "go under the chariot, beneath the cherubs; take a handful of burning coal from between the cherubs and scatter it over the city".

Jl 2:1+ [p. 1471]. (v.6)

Sound the trumpet in Zion,
give the alarm on My holy mountain!
Let all the inhabitants of the country tremble,
for the Day of Yahweh is coming,
yes, it is near.

Ex 9:24. [p. 88]. (v.7)

Yahweh rained down hail on the land of Egypt. The hail fell and lightning flashing in the midst of it, a greater storm of hail than had ever been known in Egypt.

Jl 3:3. [p. 1474]. (v.7)

I will display portents in heaven and on earth,
blood and fire and columns of smoke.

Jr 61:25. [p. 1336]. (v.8)

My quarrel is with you,
Mountain of Destruction
it is Yahweh who speaks
destroyer of the whole world
I will stretch out My hand against you
and send you trembling from the crags
and make you a mountain scorched!
Never a cornerstone will be taken from you,
never a foundation stone either,
for you will be a desert forever,
it is Yahweh who speaks.

Ex 7:20. [p. 86]. (v.8)

Moses and Aaron did as Yahweh commanded. He raised his staff, and in the sight of Pharoah and his court he struck the waters of the river and all the water in the river changed to blood.

Is 14:12. [p. 1165]. (v.10)

(See last reference of Chapter Two)

Jr 9:14. [p. 1268]. (v.10)

And so this is what Yahweh Saboath, the God of Israel says: "Now I am going to give this people wormwood for their food and poisoned water to drink ..."

Ex 10:21-23. [p. 89]. (v.12)

Then Yahweh said to Moses, "Stretch out your hand towards heaven, and let darkness, darkness so thick that it can be felt, cover the land of Egypt …"

Ezk 7:5,26. [p. 1367]. (v.13)

The Lord Yahweh says this: "Now disaster is going to follow on disaster …"

"… they will look for peace and there will be none. Disaster will follow on disaster, rumour on rumour; they will pester the prophet for a vision; the priests will be at a loss over the law, and the elders on how to advise".

Hab 2;6f. [p. 1515-6]. (v.13)

A five-fold 'trouble' enumerated here in the prophet's section on "Curses on oppressors". The reader is referred to it, but here is a list of the five 'troubles' to show how 'ancient' human nature is, now matter how 'progressive' and 'advanced' we might consider ourselves …

6. Trouble is coming to the man who amasses goods that are not his.

9. Trouble is coming to the man who grossly exploits others.

12. Trouble is coming to the man who builds a town with blood, and founds a city on crime.

15. Trouble is coming to the man who makes his neighbours drunk to look at their nakedness …

19. Trouble is coming to the man who says to the price of wood, 'Wake up!', and to the dumb stone, 'On your feet!'. [The idolatry of our present-day materialism.]

Section 9

The Ninth Chapter in the Book of Revelation
The Fifth and Sixth Trumpet
The First and Second Woe

As the Church approaches the climax in Her confrontation with the powers of evil, so the descriptions of St. John become more detailed, and the demands on a commentator more taxing, as every detail in the vision has a meaning and a Divine purpose. No wonder, then, that in this chapter Fr. Kramer takes his time guiding his readers with considerable skill through every detail of the panorama, making the task of summarizing ever so much more difficult.

But as we are also approaching the hour of the complete Revelation of the Marian Dimension within the Church, we press on toward that blessed moment, regardless of the difficulties, or of the tortuous roads that lead us to our destination, in the great consolation that evil has not the final word.

Fr. Kramer's Commentary

At the sound of the fifth Trumpet a 'fallen star' becomes visible. Not one in the act of falling, still burning bright as we witnessed earlier, but as one who has lost his Light. A great apostate bishop or priest.

A 'key' was given this star. Since it was given him, he can only use it with Divine permission. He freely uses this power to open the 'shaft' of the abyss. This scene leads Fr. Kramer to consider another 'key' and to teach by contrast.

Our Lord promised Peter: "I will give to thee the keys to the Kingdom of Heaven". The keys of the Church. The keys promised Peter for his fearless profession of Faith in the Divinity of Christ, are the emblem of supreme power and authority over the Church. They would convey possession of the whole of Divine Revelation, the Deposit of Faith, and of the perpetual privilege of being divinely guided to make unwavering and infallible decisions in matters of Faith. The mind of God would be in him always as it was at the time when he made this first 'declaration of Faith'. It entailed humility, because it required submission of the intellect and will to Christ. And the Promise also guaranteed purity of morals through the ratification of all decisions and decrees.

In the significance of the key given to the 'fallen star' we have the complete antithesis of what was promised Peter. Here we see an apostate at work. His 'key' to the shaft of the abyss is an emblem of rebellion. It leagues the 'star' with the rebellious angels, unlocked from the abyss. This key to the pit is then a sign of error, as Peter's keys are a sign of guaranteed truth.

As God revealed the truth to Peter, enabling him to teach and lead others, so the 'king of the bottomless pit' infused errors into the mind of this 'fallen star', inspiring him to teach and spread error and immorality over the world.

The Priesthood in the Church is vested with the power to suppress and subject the satanic forces through the Sacrifice of the Mass and the administering of the Seven Sacraments. But when abused, this power serves to foster and propagate evil, and to open the abyss, and envelop the earth in darkness.

This 'fallen star' is obviously some great leader of revolt against the authority of the Church, and more directly: against the Papacy itself. He is the father or shepherd of apostates from Catholicism and of rebels against the Pope, as Peter, i.e. every Pope, is the shepherd and father of Christ's followers. The inclusion by St. John of 'the key' in this vision shows that rebellion against the Papacy is a major factor in this Priest or Bishop's apostasy from the Church. With this 'key' he becomes the head of Satan's church, as Peter is the head of Christ's Church. But since the 'key of the pit' symbolizes unbelief and rebellion, whilst the 'keys of Peter' symbolize Faith, submission and obedience, the followers of the 'fallen star', once released by him from the authority of the Pope, will go their own ways, and will repudiate any authority he himself may want to exercise over them. They only use him and his 'doctrines' to become liberalized from the Church on his assumed 'authority', but once liberalized from the authority of the Church, they remain liberalized from any authority, including his, unless they will agree to it.

This is seen from the plague of 'locusts' that come out of the smoke unleashed from the bottomless pit. In the Book of Proverbs, 30:27 it is stated: "the locust has no king"! The apostate unlocks error from Hell which darkens Faith in the authority of the Church and lowers man's respect for it. But out of it came a rampage of situations and beings "he no longer was able to control".

When the 'smoke' comes in contact with conditions on earth the 'locusts' are produced, and even spread to regions not covered by the 'smoke'. They operate and are successful amongst sinners who have grown lukewarm towards the Church. They are allowed to sting them, not to kill them. All this represents spiritual torment. The 'new religion' spread by the 'star' and the locusts he cannot control, causes acute pains of conscience, which remorse, if not obeyed in a certain time, five months, will be followed by an irrevocable lapse. In their torment many adherents of the 'new religion' would like to die rather than live on in their pitiful state, apparently hoping that, on their deathbed, they can make peace with God. But God requires a conversion, which requires a grace which has been forsaken by the victims of the 'locusts' because of their alienation from the 'seal of the living God': the Baptismal and Confirmation graces.

The monstrous locusts have strange 'markings'.

- ❖ They resemble '*war horses*' equipped for battle. Signs of their determination to bring down the bastions of the Church against the forces of Hell. They use intimidation against weak and lapsed Catholics.
- ❖ "*Crowns 'like' gold ...*" Imitation gold symbolizes imitation authority arrogated by the wearers. Here it refers even more to the usurpation of a 'spiritual dominion': the audacity to force people under their earthly authority to embrace the 'new religion' and to accept them as 'heads of churches' set up by themselves without Divine jurisdiction.
- ❖ They have a '*human face*', which means they are rational creatures knowing the evil they are perpetrating.
- ❖ '*Hair like the hair of women ...*' These 'locust-princes' are effeminate, voluptuous, seekers of vain glory, which vices

produce endless enmities, rivalries, jealousies and immorality amongst themselves.

- ❖ '*Lion's teeth*'. They are cruel people, but they have not got the other characteristics of lions, but only the teeth to lacerate defenceless victims.
- ❖ '*Breastplates like iron*'. This detail shows them to be hardened against the Truth, and obstinate in their infernal intentions and activities, unwilling to listen to reason. This figure reveals them to be 'mailed against attack in debate, unwilling to be won over by reason and persuasion'.
- ❖ '*Noisy wings ...*'. This signifies great power of propaganda. Reason or logic does not rule either their speech or their manner. They 'terrorize and intimidate into silence' any opposition.
- ❖ '*Scorpion's tails ...*' The 'tail' in prophetic literature is the symbol of deceit and lying, of hypocrisy and false doctrine.. Isaias 9:15-17. The poisonous sting in the 'tails' of these monsters aptly describes the sophistry, the cunning deceit and the false conclusions, which the propagators of heresy are capable of drawing from Sacred Scripture and the Teachings of the Church, by which they mislead their dupes, terrorize them into submission, and then engender in their victims the anguish and pangs of conscience referred to above.

The whole description of this scene fits, down to the last detail, the origins and spread of Protestantism, and the unruly princes and kings of the sixteenth century who established by force, the heresies of Luther, Calvin, Zwingli and others in Europe; and those of the Anglicanism of Henry VIII and Cranmer in England. The proponents of Protestantism made false translations of the bible and then misled people into their errors by apparently proving from the 'bible' the correctness of their doctrines. Bad and weak, lax and lukewarm, indifferent, worldly and non-practising Catholics and those who had neglected to get thorough instruction in their Religion, were caught up in the new ideas and were no longer capable of extricating themselves because of their disuse of the Sacramental Fonts within the Church. Seeing the Church and the papacy through the haze and smoke of the new religion, all they could manage to see, under the 'noisy propaganda' of their new teachers, was, of course, a caricature of the Church.

I wonder what Catholic-in-the-know, reading Fr. Kramer's compelling narrative of which the above is only a summary, would not be forced to admit that, if the name of *Teilhard De Chardin* was attached to the figure 'opening the shaft of the abyss', the whole vision turns out to be a most vivid and accurate description of the *modernistic scene* of our own days ... The parallelism is uncanny, and obviously more than coincidence; and here we have another instance of a prophecy which has an immediate fulfilling as well as a more distant one. Or else, heretics are so stereotyped that they all have only one modus vivendi et operandi: only one way of 'making their presence felt', no matter where, or in what age they live.

But there is one major difference which prevents the above from being applied exclusively to our own days: a difference of 'time'. Apocalyptic time. And we do well not to rush ahead of the 'time table' set by God Himself. Which means we accept Fr. Kramer's erudite findings, which, he assures us, are shared by many commentators he has consulted, and we go along with the observation that he has given us an accurate description of the sixteenth century Reformation. If, then, there is a strong resemblance with our own times, this is only because heretics cannot be but stereotyped; and because falling away from the Truth at any time, not only marks a man for his own days, but for all times.

As we saw, the word 'key' used by St. John inspired Fr. Kramer to a convincing comparison between the 'fallen star's usurped powers of corruption' and the divinely guaranteed power of the papacy. Following this lead, I would like to put before the reader another comparison between two 'keys:' one, the 'key to the shaft of the bottomless pit', and the other, the key we are told by the Apocalypse is held by Christ: '*the Key of David*'.

We recall from Chapter Four, Section IV, that 'the Key of David' held by Christ, i.e. the 'key' to the Redemption, is a delicate reference by the Holy Spirit to Our Blessed Lady. Her 'Fiat' helped unlock the 'door in Heaven' through which Christ could come down to earth, and unlocked the door to the Sanctuary of Her virginal Womb at the Incarnation. Of this Key it is written: "He who opens and no one shall shut, He who shuts and no one shall open". How forcefully we are reminded of those words here, when 'the smoke of Satan' is belching forth from an opened shaft and the true lovers of Christ gather around Him to seek asylum. With this Key, no doubt, Christ opened for all His children the door to the shelter of 'the Marian Dimension' in His Holy Church. And closed the door after them, shutting out the 'smoke' and the 'locusts', since 'no one can open that sacred Door'. With Her, all who wished to enter, would be safe.

Great devotion to Our Lady, then, became more and more a hallmark of holiness in those troublesome times, and was pursued, taught and practised by all those who, far from wishing to cut themselves off from active participation in the affairs of the age, discovered to their great consolation, that the 'Marian Dimension' is a 'climate of sanity and sanctity', which allows one to live in one's very own times, yet with a certain immunity against its temptations and perversities.

Are not these the times, in which the victory in a great sea battle, the Battle of Lepanto against the Turks in 1571, was attributed to the *Power of the Holy Rosary* by a Pope and Saint of that period, Pope St. Pius V? Are not we reminded of this power of the Holy Rosary, when, according to the commentary of Fr. Kramer, the victims of the onslaught of Protestantism 'had about five months', in which the acute pains of conscience compelled them to seek help from God?

The number 'five' here reminds us (and no doubt was meant to remind them), of two famous "Fives" in the devotional life of the Church: the *Five Decades of the Rosary*, and the *Five Sacred Wounds of our Holy Redeemer*, which are combined together in the *Five Sorrowful Mysteries*. If these victims succeeded in praying the Holy Rosary for those five months, and meditated on the Passion and Death of Our Blessed Saviour, according to the Apocalypse then, they would have been saved from apostasy from the Catholic Faith. *Five months of Prayer* against an eternity to regret the neglect …

But, would it be possible to make all this even more compelling? Can we link those 'five months' of the Apocalypse *directly* to Our Lady? That is, are we able to quote Our Blessed Lady *verbatim* as having used those exact words: "Five Months", somewhere in connection with salvation? If so, then the use of exactly the same time span here in the Apocalypse in connection with the saving of souls, must be considered a strong indication, that the Holy Spirit is once again revealing to us in the Book of Revelation the existence of the 'Marian Dimension' in the Catholic Church in the time of the Reformation.

The answer to our questions is, of course, our Heavenly Mother's promise at Fatima of the *Five First Saturdays of Five Consecutive Months.*

We are tremendously privileged of having the full extent of the Marian Dimension within the Church revealed to us by Our Blessed Mother Herself. But that does not make Her concern any less for the weak and poor Catholics of the Reformation, who were misled and often coerced by the Protestant revolt. And how many are there today who show no gratitude and appreciation, and who refuse to make full use of the graces and promises extended to us with so much love! God still loved all those duped by the turmoil of the Sixteenth Century. As a singular grace He allowed a part of the Apocalypse, the times of the 'flying eagle' in Chapter 8, to be identified, as we saw, with the days of two great Saints by an extraordinary miracle.

Christians coming after that could know that they would be the people of the next phase of which it was revealed, that those who had not lived up to the demands of the 'Seal of God', that is to their

Baptismal and Confirmation graces, would be stung; and would suffer the painful consequences of that sting for *five months* ... Many would have realised, with the help of the Holy Spirit, that extra prayers were recommended. And they knew what prayers were recommended especially now that the Papacy, aware of the ravages caused by the Protestant Revolt, held up the saying of the Holy Rosary as an efficacious means to counteract the onslaught, and to obtain healing graces and pardon from God through the powerful intercession of His Holy Mother.

Knowing that Catholics of future ages would benefit tremendously from the 'Five First Saturdays', God allowed the earlier people in the same dire straight a similar option to be realised in the same time span: to say the Rosary, recommended by the Holy See and rewarded by a stupendous victory; to meditate on the Passion of Our Lord; and to receive the Sacraments as a result of their prayers, which then would squash, in a period of some five months, any desire to go over to, or stay any longer in, the 'new religion'.

This should finally remove any lingering hesitation many non-Catholics still harbour against devotion to Our Blessed Lady, as if it is something Catholics do 'in isolation', contrary to Jesus Christ. For what has been said here most strongly confirms what we discovered earlier on: that *Marian Catholics are Eucharistic Catholics!* Great devotion to Our Blessed Lady leads to God. Leads to the Sacraments and the frequent reception of Holy Communion. And what could be more pleasing to Jesus, Our Eucharistic Lamb and King? ...

Fr. Kramer's Commentary on the second half of Chapter 9

St. John announces the end of one woe threatened by the eagle. The lukewarm and proud are cleared out of the Church in the countries struck by the first woe. Two more woes are to follow. The next one will bring calamities upon the whole world: upon good and bad alike, and will separate them more completely in all countries.

At the sound of the Sixth Trumpet the Seer hears a single voice from the Four Horns of the Golden Altar. Since the Golden Altar represents the Religious Orders in the Church, the one voice must then signify a unanimous declaration of all the Religious that the Church is ready to meet the new and fiercest onslaught in Her whole history up until now.

After the establishment of Protestantism in Northern Europe and England, the Council of Trent reiterated, defined and expressed in clear language the Dogmas of the Church for all times. It was mainly left to the Religious Orders and Congregations to carry the renewal in catechetics, education and other works of mercy to all parts of the world, and this was done with great success and vigour. But the speeding up of the Christianisation of the world forced the Devil to even greater and more devious and forceful opposition then had hitherto been the case. Four bad spirits had to be let loose. They come from the region of the Euphrates whence come the enemies of God's people. Since the order comes indirectly from God, it is consoling to know, no matter how vehement and even bloody the opposition may turn out, it can only do what God permits it to do, and it will be forced to ultimately *serve His ends* like everything else. The true director of world affairs remains the Eucharistic Lamb from the Sanctuary of His Church.

The text gives no indication about the interval of time between the first and second woe. It will be a time of wars developing into world revolutions that will deluge the whole world in carnage and bloodshed. The three-and-one-half year reign of Antichrist will be its climax.

St. John abruptly gives the number of killers appearing on the scene, which is two hundred million horsemen. The revelation seems to startle the Seer, for he adds, as if expecting scepticism from his readers over so large a number of cavalry in the world, "I heard the number of them". The number either indicates a long session of wars in which vast armies are engaged, or a universal revolution and overthrow of governments with incessant guerilla fighting, when everybody carries weapons for self-defence, and rapine and murder become universal.

The colours reveal the characters of the riders: fire is the symbol of hatred; flame-coloured smoke that of blasphemy; and sulphur represents rebellion against God and His Law. The horsemen are not the locusts of the first woe. The riders are distinct from the horses they ride. The men have on their armour only the colours of the substances emitted from the mouths of the horses. But this shows how deeply imbued they themselves are with these satanic qualities in their own minds and hearts.

These horses and riders again execute the Judgements of God. The horses would then represent the *organisations and institutions* that are filled with satanic hatred against God, against Christ and

His Church. The riders *rule and direct* those institutions and forces, in the hope of gaining universal power.

The horses have heads of lions, which property relates them closely to 'the Beast' which has a mouth of a lion. The monsters have thus great powers of *propaganda* for the overthrow of governments in preparation for the rule of the Beast.

The fire, the smoke and sulphur issuing from the mouths of the horses will bring death to one third of mankind. Hatred of god and fellow-men is the efficient cause. The 'institutions' will voice their sentiments in blasphemous propaganda against God and all Revealed Religion with the direct aim for, and result of, a universal rebellion against His Law, refusal to keep His Commandments and a worldwide surrender to wickedness and immorality. St. John calls the fire, the smoke and the sulphur three distinct plagues.

As men still sin against God's Sovereignty so shall they also sin against the moral order. The final verse, verse 21, points to the Christian world. After the slaughter of one third of mankind is ended, the Christian world shall still be given to murders, adultery, divorce, birth-control, false beliefs, fornication, dishonesty, secret addictions to witchcraft, devil worship and fortune telling. Deceit and hypocrisy shall go unchecked. Dishonesty and graft in business shall be almost universal.

From the vast amount of texts in the Old Testament we know that this was the state of Israel just before the Judgements struck all countries in communication with Israel. Christendom is now hopelessly divided by heresy and schism. The rest of mankind is satisfied to live in religious indifference. All resent any attempts to enlighten them, although they listen eagerly to heretical teachings and to all slanders against the Catholic Church. By continually tempting the Catholics to a compromise with false standards and teachings, and even by leading the Clergy away from the strictness of virtue into worldliness, the wicked will hasten their own judgements *as the Judgements once again will begin at the House of God.*

This will do to show, how vast even a mere detail of the complete Panorama becomes, if we are close enough to it. According to Fr. Kramer, we still find ourselves 'in the ninth chapter', because we are still 'in the Second Woe', which means that he, and for that matter we, would not be distant enough to take in and comprehend the meaning of every detail; or even of the 'whole' itself. We may be able to explain the 'part' which has already come to pass, but explaining the 'part' which is still in the future would then result in guesswork. There is no denying that Father's explanations here, although consistent, are becoming unusually vague and groping.

This, then, must be the point, *where the ignoring of the clear existence of the Marian Dimension within the Apocalypse* finally catches up with even as fascinating an expert as Fr. Kramer. The 'second woe' extends over a number of chapters of the Book of Revelation, which means that we are not forced to consider ourselves locked in the Ninth Chapter simply because the 'second woe' is not finished.

This 'woe' culminates with the reign of 'the Beast', which is the subject-matter of Chapters Thirteen and Fourteen. If it is possible to consider ourselves past Chapter Nine, then, I am sure, a better fist could be made of the rich detail St. John supplies us with to enlarge our understanding of its important contents.

There are a number of things Fr. Kramer has failed to develop. Since they are all in the past, we should be able to throw some light on them.

(i) St. John clearly states 'that the first woe has passed'. Since 'protestantism' is still with us a meaning has to be found for this statement.
(ii) St. John's reference to 'the river Euphrates'.
(iii) 'The four bound spirits who apparently knew the hour, the day, the month and the year of their release'.
(iv) 'For their tails are like serpents with heads ...'

I will not develop these references point by point, but simply state what I have to say as a foundation for my main concern: 'the Marian Dimension'.

Mgr. George F. Dillon, DD, in his classic book: *The War of Antichrist with the Church and with Christian Civilization*, (1885), made the following remark at the opening of his second chapter:

> "In order then to comprehend thoroughly the nature of the conspiracy, it will be necessary to go back to the opening of the last century and contemplate the rise and advance of the Atheism and Anti-Christianity which it now spreads rapidly through the earth. As that century opened it disclosed a world suffering from a multitude of evils. *The so-called Reformation*, which arose and continued to progress during the two preceding centuries *had well nigh run its course.* The principle of private judgement introduced in apparent

> zeal for the pure worship and doctrine of Christ, *had ended* in leaving no part of the teaching of Christ unchallenged. It had rendered His Divinity disbelieved in, and His very existence doubted by many who yet called themselves His followers."

According to this, the Reformation, at the beginning of the Eighteenth Century, was a *spent force*: 'the first woe' had passed. It had devoured all who wished; it had started to sprout 'children of its own' and had left the Church stronger, more united and young. We have entered the age of Voltaire, who already in his one person, embodies everything Fr. Kramer described for us earlier. It was Voltaire who outlined for his numerous disciples, [as became known from the correspondence of Frederik II, e.g. one letter dated August 13, 1775] how to suppress the Jesuits *and all Religious Orders* and to secularize their goods. Even as late as 1812, all Religious Orders were dissolved in Germany. Earlier, to avoid a serious threat of schism, Pope Clement XIV had dissolved the Jesuits in 1773. No wonder, then, that it was the 'golden altar', which commanded the release of the 'four spirits bound at the Euphrates'.

This necessitates the combination of the following distinct particulars:

- ❖ The 'Euphrates' is not 'the four evil spirits', but their origin.
- ❖ And the 'Euphrates' is not 'Protestantism', for that woe had already passed. The language of St. John is pretty clear on this.

- ❖ The 'four evil spirits' were released (in the nineteenth century?) AFTER a command from the 'golden altar', (late eighteenth century, somewhere around the time of the French Revolution), necessitated by the discovery of a wicked 'Euphrates' (begin eighteenth century) trying to suppress the Religious Orders (late eighteenth century, notably 1774),
- ❖ which 'Euphrates' is not synonymous with the Reformation.

The most important thing to do now is to discover what the Holy Spirit had in Mind when He made St. John reveal *a historical event after the Reformation* under the name of the river Euphrates.

The entity covered by this symbolic name is not a person, but a system, inimical to the Church, capable of unleashing 'evil spirits' which in time would gather together an army of staggering proportions.

To get a line on this 'Euphrates', we have to turn to the Word of God in Holy Scripture, since it seems to be impossible to get our information elsewhere. No better place to go to anyway!

The 'great river Euphrates' has a distinguished beginning in the Bible: it is one of the four great rivers which have their origin 'from the stream in the middle of the Garden', [Gen. 2:14]. Then, still in Genesis, God decreed that the Euphrates would constitute the distant boundary (north-east) for Abraham's inheritance, [Gen. 15:18]. Hereafter, when it gets a sparse mention in the Bible, it is nearly always as that mysterious, far-away '*demarcation line*' beyond which lay territory not to be coveted by the Jews. When they eventually did cross this river, it was as captives and slaves, on transit to the Babylonian Captivity ...

From times immemorial the Jews have had a penchant for 'secret societies', where they were introduced to 'mysteries and knowledge' which invariably caused them to stray away from the service of Yahweh into idolatry and immorality. In their own religion there was a '*demarcation line*' across which they were not to transgress, and beyond which lay nothing they should covet. This forbidden territory of knowledge exerted a strong appeal on them (as the tree of knowledge of good and evil had on Eve) because of its secret promise of 'power'. 'Baal' was this dividing line, this '*spiritual Euphrates*', between loyalty, love and service of Yahweh on one side, or entering into territory across this line, with empty promises of immediate power and fulfilment, but at the expense of alienation from Truth and Redemption. 'Baal' was religion 'perverted at its source', as James Michener so aptly describes it in his absorbing book: "The Source".

Eighteenth century Freemasonry, to a T, so accurately fits this description, that we do not have to look much further for explanations, to make it correspond with St. John's function of the river Euphrates in this part of Chapter Nine.

Spawned in London in 1717 with the active cooperation of Voltaire, then in exile from France, as the Grand Lodge of London, it was soon brought to France, where in 1725 the famous mother Lodge in Paris was founded by Lord Derwentwater, to become the Grand Orient of France. But the Bride of the Lamb of God was alerted by the Holy Spirit, ready to warn her children:

"Lying is their rule, Satan is their God, and shameful deeds their sacrifice", so wrote Pope Pius VIII in 1829.

His successor, Pope Gregory XVI, compares the secret societies to "a sink, in which are congregated and intermingled all the sacrileges, infamy, blasphemy which are contained in the most abominable heresies". (1832)

"Those baneful secret sects which have come forth from the darkness for the ruin and devastation of both Church and State", wrote Pope Pius IX in 1846.

Etc. Etc.

"*Pollution of Divine Revelation at its Source,*" is the most apt description we can give, then, to Freemasonry, to this 'Euphrates': this 'line of demarcation' between Revealed Religion in the Catholic Church and the 'mysteries of Satan' at the other side.

This 'Euphrates' then, held tied to itself all the final evils which Satan would unleash as truly inspired by him 'at the hour, the day, the month and the year' set aside for this purpose, as a veritable time bomb ticking away until the preset moment of its explosion, with the release of the 200,000,000 fragments: the 'human agents', all stamped with the birth mark of their origin: '*pollution of Revealed Truth at its very source*'.

The 'four spirits' *thus marked* are Communism, Humanism, Evolution and Modernism. Of each one of these it is possible to pinpoint the very moment their 'charter' or 'manifesto' was produce and 'revealed' to the world. And it is not hard to see that, between them, these deadly systems would be able to muster 200 million active proponents and adherents.

In the light of St. John's Revelation 'that the spirits were bound at the Euphrates', which may now take to mean that these four systems are intimately bound up with Freemasonry, it is of greatest importance to know that Adam Weishaupt, the apostate priest and father of the 'illuminati', himself wrote "The Constitution for Atheistic Communism", clearly linking the 'Euphrates' of Freemasonry with one of its 'spiritual hybrids', Communism. Each one of the other three can be traced, with equal certitude, to the same polluted river.

Since Socialism is nothing but a euphemism for Communism, e.g. USSR, it does not deserve to receive a separate mention as one of the 'four spirits' derived from Freemasonry.

These four enemies of the Church are most formidable, and their multi-million number of promoters is impressive. In the modern world everything seems to be going their way, under their control: the press, the media, the schools, the colleges, the universities, governments, finance, religion. Even within the Catholic Church they can boast of having cardinals, bishops, priests, nuns, brothers, catholic laypeople, editors of weeklies and periodicals, composers of catechetics courses, lecturers in seminaries, theologians, philosophers firmly in their grip of iron; actively cooperating with their devilish plans and destruction. Still it is not enough. For one, it is written: 'see the second woe has passed ...'. Communism and marxism will come to an end. Humanism will be a spent force. Evolution will be a dead issue. Modernism nothing but a dirty word - a thing of the past. No longer will people be able to sin in the name of an '*ism*', a system. They will finally be forced to stand before God with the Beast and declare:

> "I sin because I want to. *I will not serve*. I will not turn away from my evil works. All the enemies of the past, all the spent forces: Paganism, Barbarism, Heresies, Schisms, Reformation, Enlightenment, Freemasonry, Rationalism, Humanism, Evolution, Communism, Modernism have proved of no avail and brought me to this final decision, this ultimate stand: I sin because I like to. Because I want Satan for my god and father. I will only serve him. I want him to rule the world. To destroy the Church. *I defy you* ..."

And we can see that this ultimate in evil, this total godlessness, this fury of moral, spiritual and material destruction, this utter blindness and complete darkness is rapidly gaining a foothold across the face of the earth.

And still it will not be enough ...

This force may ultimately even manage 'to abolish the Perpetual Sacrifice for a time, two times and half a time', (Dn. 8: 11), the exact time span allotted to the reign of the Beast. It may even be given the power 'to conquer the Saints' (Apoc. 13; 7) ...

Yet it will all be of no avail ...

For, from times immemorial, THE Enmity has not been put by God between Satan and Himself; *but between the Woman and the Serpent, and between Her Seed and his. And SHE shall crush his head* ...

Now that the '200 million horsemen': Communists, Humanists, Evolutionists, Modernists, are rapidly hastening the day for this final stand, this ultimate in evil and defiance – Antichrist – they are also hastening the fulfilment of that First Prophecy in Paradise. For here, in this last chapter before the full manifestation of the Marian Dimension within the Church in all its Glory, are we able to detect, that God has this spectacular *confrontation* still uppermost in Mind, and that the long interval of time in between has done nothing to weaken the original resolve or precision. For the final part of this chapter in the Apocalypse bristles with references to Paradise, and, far from drawing our uncomprehending gaze to a mysterious future peopled with millions of evil doers, it is taking us right back to that clear and momentous Prophecy at the beginning...

- ❖ With the word '*Euphrates*' God takes us here once again to the 'centre of Paradise': Gen. 2: 14.
- ❖ With the words '*the tail of a serpent With Head*' He brings us face to face with THE serpent in Paradise: Gen. 3: 13.
- ❖ And with the expression '*200 million serpent's tails with heads*' He can only remind us of His omnipotent words spoken to Satan in Paradise and spanning all these ages: '*and your seed*'. Gen. 3:15.

Three clear references to what happened 'in Paradise'.

After centuries of intermediate steps, all disclosed, as we saw, in this most powerful book of St. John; Evil has finally reached 'the pollution at the source of Revelation itself'. So God forcibly reminds us what was actually said by Him 'at the very source of Revelation'. And if here, with an unmistakable vision, He Divinely reveals to us the existence of 'Satan's' seed' in the Apocalypse, and takes us back 'to the centre of Paradise', then it is also clearly His intention to reveal to us once and for all that that "other seed mentioned in the centre of Paradise" also exists right here in this very chapter: '*the seed of the Woman, the Marian Dimension*'.

For it would be impossible to accept that God, Who only has Good in view, would take us here right back 'to the centre of Paradise' with the mention of the word 'Euphrates', would forcibly remind us, through the images used here by St. John, of Satan and 'his seed' without wanting to remind us even stronger of the One He Himself opposed against Satan and his seed: '*the Woman and Her seed*'.

With such a forceful indication of the existence of 'the Marian Dimension' at this point in the Apocalypse, and of God's clear intention to draw our attention to it, we may expect that, from now on, this unbreakable unity of the Marian Dimension with the Catholic Church will break out into the open in the only existing record of the infallible history of the Church: in the Apocalypse of St. John.

And what form will 'the Marian Dimension' have taken by then?

Neither God nor His Church have been slow in answering that question. For, at the beginning of the reign of Freemasonry, that is, as we saw, at the beginning of the pollution of Revolution at its source, God had already called up in His Church one of the greatest Marian Saints who ever lived, *St. Louis Grignion de Montfort.* His treatise on 'The True Devotion', discovered, as he predicted, a century after his death, and in 1853 officially declared free from all error, has shaped the style and the efficiency of the 'seed of the Woman' *destined to meet the fury of hell before and during the reign of the beast.* Their 'total consecration' was clearly meant by God to give to 'the Woman' the most devoted children, the most effective instruments She needed in Her final battle with the one She was to crush ...

Old Testament References in Chapter 9

Is 14:12. [p. 1165]. (v.1)

See last reference of Ch. 2.

Gn 19:28. [p. 36]. (v.2)

Rising early in the morning Abraham went to the place where he had stood before Yahweh, and looking towards Sodom and Gomorrah, and across all the plain, he saw the smoke rising from the land, like smoke from a furnace ...

Ex 19:18. [p. 102]. (v.2)

The mountain of Sinai was entirely wrapped in smoke, because Yahweh had descended in the form of fire. Like smoke from a furnace the smoke went up and the whole mountain shook violently.

Ex 10:12,15. [p. 89]. (v.3)

Then Yahweh said to Moses, 'Stretch out your hand over the land of Egypt to bring the locusts. Let them invade the land of Egypt and devour all its greenstuff, all that the hail has left'...

Ws 16:9. [p. 1028]. (v.3)

... since the bites of locusts and flies proved fatal to them (i.e. to our enemies) and no remedy could be found to save them, - and well they deserved to be punished by such creatures.

Jl 1:1-2:17. [p. 1469-72]. (v.3-5)

Readers are referred to these two chapters.

Ezk 9:6. [p.370] (v.4)

'... kill and exterminate them all. But do not touch anyone with a cross on his forehead. Begin at My sanctuary'.

Jb 3:21. [p.730]. (v.6)

[Why give life to those bitter of heart],
Who long for a death that never comes,
and hunt for it more than for buried treasure?

Jl 2:4. [p.1471]. (v.7)

They look like horses,
like chargers they gallop on.

Jl 1:6. [p.1469]. (v.8)

For a nation has invaded my country,
mighty and innumerable;
its teeth are the teeth of lions,
it has the fangs of a lioness.

Jl 2:5. [p.1471]. (v.9)

With a racket like the clatter of chariots
they hurtle over the mountain tops.

Ezk 7:5. [p.1367]. (v.12)

'Now disaster is going to follow disaster ...'

Ex 30:1-3. [p.116]. (v.13)

You must make an altar on which to burn incense; you are to make it out of acacia wood ... Its horns are to be of one piece with it. The top of it, its surrounding sides, and its horns, are to be plated with pure gold, and decorated with a gold moulding all round.

Jb 41:10-13. [p.776]. (v.17)

From his [Leviathan's] mouth come fiery torches,

sparks of fire fly out of it.
His nostrils belch smoke
like a cauldron boiling on the fire.

Am 4:6+ [p.1482]. (v.20-21)

In referring to this passage of the prophet Amos, the Apocalypse is indicating that an impasse has been reached. For it is here that the prophet enumerates how God, as a Father, has punished His children in order that they should return to Him, without avail. Other references in Holy Scripture to this sad state of affairs are numerous, and are listed at the end of this passage. v.6 Famine, v.7 Drought, v.9 Fire and Locusts, v.10 Sword and War, v.11 Earthquakes and Natural Disasters.

See also,

Deut 8:5+;	Levit. 26:14-39;	Deut. 28:15-68
and		
Is. 9:12;	Jerem. 2:30;	Hosea 7:10;
42: 25;	5:3;	Zeph. 3:2,7;
Haggai 2:17;	Rev. 9:20, 21;	Exodus 7-11;
	16:9,11	

Is 17:8. [p.1169]. (v.20)

That day, man will look to his Creator and his eyes will turn to the Holy One of Israel. He will no longer look after the altars, his own handiwork, nor gaze at what his hands have made: the sacred poles and the solar pillars.

Dn 5:4. [p.1434]. (v.20)

They drank their wine and praised their gods of gold and silver, or bronze and iron, of wood and stone ...

Dn 5:23. [p.1434]. (v.20)

' ... You have praised gods of gold and silver, or bronze and iron, of wood and stone, which cannot either see, hear or understand; but you have given no glory to the true God Who holds your breath and all your fortunes in His Hands ...

Ps 135:15-17. [p.918]. (v.20)

... whereas pagans' idols, in silver and gold,
products of human skill,
have mouths, but never speak,
eyes, but never see,
ears, but never hear,
and not a breath in their mouth.
THEIR MAKERS WILL END UP LIKE THEM
AND SO WILL ANYONE WHO RELIES ON THEM ...

Section 10

The Tenth Chapter in the Book of Revelation
The Seven Thunders. The Oath.
The Open Booklet.

Fr. Kramer's Commentary

By the time the prophecies of this 'open booklet' will go into fulfilment, the global evil institutions, crawling all over with 200 million followers of Satan, '*Satan's seed*', will be fully operational, working at peak capacity. Abortion on demand, legalized homosexuality, easy divorce, contraception, lewd advertising, pornography, sex education in schools, child abuse, riots, murder, abductions and rape will have spread to all the countries of the earth, 'Truth will be flung to the ground and trampled underfoot' (Dn 8:10-12), might will be right; the poor, the sick and weak will be oppressed, the ignorant taken advantage of.

Before the great Angel swears on oath 'that there will be no more delay in the consummation of God's mystery as He has announced to His servants the prophets', he roared something to which the 'seven thunders' added their own voices. But St. John was to keep the words of the seven thunders secret. This means he understood what was said, which in turn means that the Church knows it too, but that it will be revealed by God in His own time to whom He will give the Light of Understanding.

'Thunder', as we have been told earlier, signifies 'the highest authority in the Church'. 'The Seven' can mean here several Popes making dogmatic pronouncements, or an Ecumenical Council, or even seven famous encyclicals. The Seven Thunders will undoubtedly strengthen the faithful and loyal clergy in their belief and practices, expel all who are addicted to corruption in morals or doctrine, and will manifest the unwavering stand of the Church in opposition to the then prevailing maxims of the world.

The 'Mystery of Iniquity' (Thess. 2:7), the mystery of its origin and spread, the mystery of its final defeat and the mystery of the preservation and continuation of the Church rising above the conflagration, which will totally consume both evil and the evildoers, are all such that they cannot be outlined in one vision or made understandable in one lesson. This Truth has various consequences.

* For one, as is so graphically shown here by the 'eating of the scroll', God's Revelations need study, contemplation and the Supernatural Light obtained from God in prayer. A 'first and casual acquaintance' may be sweet and consoling, like the revelation by the Angel, just announced, that the wicked will get their just reward and that their will be an end to iniquity. But once God's Truth has had time to be 'digested', it may reveal aspects which may taste very bitter. It is consoling to know that the Church will be triumphant, but bitter to know the price at which that victory will have to be bought: the direst persecutions for the Church, the plagues to be inflicted by God to be borne by both the wicked and the just, the sacrifices of countless precious lives, the most horrifying chastisements for the wicked, many of whom would be near relatives or friends of the just, and the apostasy and damnation of so many weak and timid souls ...

But although some aspects of the message he received are sealed for the time being, St. John nevertheless is commanded to keep on prophesying 'to many nations and tongues and peoples and kings ...'. Not all is gloom and foreboding. There is a lot to be learned. There is a lot to be done. Not only are many going to be martyred: many will also survive and carry the Church through. All this brings us to a second consequence to come from the complexity of the mystery:

* 'Human language must traverse the same ground several times to depict the many phases of the supreme conflict in separate scenes before it can unravel the final outcome into which all events in this grand drama converge'. (Fr. Kramer). This may call for repetitions of visions, under different aspects, or even anticipation of one aspect to highlight something else. E.g. the scene of the next chapter, Chapter Eleven, depicts something during the 'reign of the Beast', whereas we are not formally introduced to its existence until Chapter Thirteen. This reinforces the previously received call by the Holy Spirit: not only to have a taste of God's revelation, but to digest it - to ponder over it.

It also means that the one historical event can find itself considered under different aspects in more than one chapter of the Apocalypse.

Is it possible to let 'the Marian Dimension' shed ever more light on both visions of this chapter in Revelation, the 'Seven Thunders' and the 'eating of the little scroll'?

A great, public and universal manifestation by God of Our Blessed Lady is close at hand; and with it the final and complete unveiling of the existence of the Marian Dimension within the Church.

Since this unveiling involves Apparitions, Dogmatic Definitions and extensive Doctrine by an Ecumenical Council, and if this Chapter Ten does speak about 'Thunder, i.e. about 'dogmatic definitions' in the Church, and since the last two 'dogmatic definitions' were *Marian Dogmas*, it is now certain that a combination of the Marian Dimension with the Supreme Teaching Authority in the Church: 'Thunder', *has occurred in this time*, and may be spoken of here in Chapter Ten. Let us now investigate if this is so. And if this is the case, then it is certain that a Marian Dimension cannot fail to make *both* scenes in this chapter much more lucid, revealing the existence of a close relationship between our own times and this Chapter Ten.

I. The 'Marian Dimension' and the 'Seven Thunders'

Fr. Kramer's erudition in these matters informs us that the 'seven thunders' could be several popes making pronouncements on a particular matter; or they could be encyclicals, or they could be the voice of an Ecumenical Council. There is a marvellous way of combining all this as follows:

Since according to the chronological sequence of the Apocalypse, we have arrived at the 'second woe', the 'seven thunders' could be seven popes during the time of the 'four evil spirits': Communism, Evolution, Humanism and Modernism, unleashed from the 'Euphrates': Freemasonry. They are: Pius IX, Leo XIII, St. Pius X, Benedict XV, Pius XI, Pius XII, John XIII. These are the same seven popes who reigned in between two great Ecumenical Councils: Vatican I and Vatican II. In their reign we have two great Marian Dogmas: Immaculate Conception and Assumption; and two great Marian Apparitions: Lourdes and Fatima. And to top it all off: at the beginning of their reign, Pope Pius IX, and also at the other end, Pope John XXIII, we have *Two Great Secrets* revealed to the Church, but kept 'sealed' thereafter: *La Salette and the third Secret of Fatima.* If this is no coincidence, then God is clearly revealing to us that this chapter has some bearing on our own times.

But we know from many other sources that the times we live in enjoy the *complete Revelation* of the existence of the Marian Dimension in Time!

- ❖ We have had the Definition of two great Marian Dogmas;
- ❖ we have had two great Marian Apparitions, Lourdes and Fatima;
- ❖ we have had the teachings of the Second Vatican Council on Mary and Her relation with the Church; and
- ❖ we have had the canonization of St. Louis Grignion de Montfort, putting thereby the Church's seal of approval on his Marian doctrine of 'total consecration'.

All this makes it appear that both Chapter Ten: the chapter on the Dogmatic Teaching on Our Blessed Lady, as well as Chapter Twelve: the chapter of the Great Apparitions, reveal the two aspects of the complete Revelation by Almighty God of Our Blessed Lady's role in the History of the Church. Both chapters are intimately related and depict our present-day times.

If then the Marian Dimension is needed to throw considerable light on the meaning of the first part of this present Chapter Ten, and this first part, as we saw, has a bearing on our times, *then Chapter Ten is already and integral part of the full revelation of Chapter Twelve* and must be considered the beginning and anticipation of it.

> [**NOTE.** This becomes even more clear when we see in the next chapter, Chapter Eleven, that we are dealing with events which take place under the 'reign of the Beast' with whom we only become officially acquainted in Chapter Thirteen, (that is, past *Chapter Twelve*), and when once again, it will be the Marian Dimension, which will explain this 'anticipation of events' much more fully and satisfactorily, thereby showing that Chapter Eleven also is an integral part of this whole panorama of God's complete Revelation of Mary in Time: the Marian Dimension. If Chapter Eleven deal with events not officially met with until Chapter Thirteen, and if Chapter Twelve is needed to explain Chapter Thirteen, then it is obviously God's Will that Chapter Eleven is explained in the light of Chapters Ten AND Twelve ... And here in Chapter Ten we are urged to ponder these things.]

We may be able to draw a few conclusions here.

1. Chapter Ten coexists with the turbulent events of the Second Woe: the rise of Communism, Humanism and Evolu-

tion, all clearly part of nineteenth century history. *But the Church is at the centre of history, and the centre of the Church is the Eucharistic Lamb.* From the Church's point of view, then, the greatest event of the nineteenth century is the dogmatic definition of the Immaculate Conception, and Our Lady's acknowledgement of that four years later with Her series of Apparitions in Lourdes. If, by the Will of God, 'Lourdes' is not yet the overt subject-matter of Chapter Ten, then at least its veiled existence makes its presence strongly felt. That's why the actual subject-matter came much more to life when the Supernatural Light of Catholic Faith in the Marian Dimension was applied to it.

2. If our times enjoy the full Revelation of the existence of the Marian Dimension within the Catholic Church, and if the Apocalypse is a true reflection of the history of that Church, then the Marian Dimension MUST exist in the Apocalypse, and we were on safe ground, not only in our investigations, but also in the use we made of that existence to throw Light on the text itself. On the other hand, if it is revealed to exist as an integral part of the Church in the Apocalypse, then it must in Time also be an integral part of the Church Christ founded.
3. Since the Marian Dimension is fully alive and active in the Apocalypse, and has been gloriously revealed in *time,* then this glorious revelation must also exist somewhere in the Apocalypse, and our times should then see themselves reflected in that Chapter. The actual manifestation in Time took more than a century: from the Dogmatic Definition of

the Immaculate Conception in 1854 to the full Mariology of the Second Vatican Council in 'Lumen Gentium', 1964. This may account for its extension over two chapters in the Book of Revelation, Chapters Ten and Twelve. Since the full manifestation by God of His Holy Mother in the latter times involved dogmatic definitions, official teaching and Apparitions, it is quite likely, that *the teachings of the Church*: the two Marian Dogmas and the Conciliar Documents are represented by the 'Thunder' in Chapter Ten, whereas the *Two Great Apparitions*: Lourdes and Fatima, are taken together in Chapter Twelve.

II. The 'Marian Dimension' and the 'eating of the scroll'

As already discussed above, God's revelation of the Truth about the climax of iniquity, and how it is going to be dealt with before the final triumph of the Church, needs contemplation and study and prayer, and not just a casual acquaintance. If the pain and the sorrow, the bitterness and agony of it all have been squarely met in prayer and meditation, then there is less likelihood that the actual undergoing of the 'baptism of fire and blood' will dampen the enthusiasm which a casual euphoria of 'all will be well' could bring. The times we live in are bad, and require, to an unusual degree, virtues like prudence, perseverance and fortitude, and the acquisition of the Gifts of the Holy Spirit even in children, which will only become habitual after some pretty advanced training not usually found in the ordinary, run-of-the-mill Christian life. This takes us back to the gift of God to His Church, discovered in the previous chapter of the Apocalypse: *'The True Devotion' of St. Louis de Montfort.* The 'total consecration' to which it leads, not only engages the special love and protection of the Mother of God, but also trains the soldier of Christ in the acquisition of the Virtues and Gifts necessary for great fidelity to the Church and Her Teaching, and for the safeguarding of all souls entrusted to one's care. This Marian devotion fully meets the requirements of this chapter: not only of tasting the scroll, but eating and digesting it, and finding ways and means of adequately coping with its bitterness...

* The Church is ready. She is facing the final battle with 'the Beast' with resignation and confidence. Even if, of this final battle, it is written that 'the Saints will be delivered into its hands, and it will conquer them'. For, when this final battle is over, and the Beast lies smitten and crushed at Her feet, *She will be the only one left over on earth.* All evil will have spent itself and will have vanished. Even of the '200 million horsemen', the emissaries of 'the four evil spirits', it is written: 'the second woe has passed'.

The final persecution will be universal and terrible, but persecutions have never been considered by Christ or the Church as a 'plague', or a 'scourge'. For it is a holy 'Baptism', as Christ called it, in which countless sinners and persecutors are washed clean. Martyrdom, according to Christ to His most trusted friends, is not something to be feared, but neither should it be presumptuously provoked.

* The Church is ready, for She has the Eucharistic Lamb, the True Ruler of the universe, the One who directs everything to His final ends.

* The Church is ready, for given to Her, at the foot of the cross, was She who has been appointed by the Father in Paradise to be victorious. Right from the opening pages of the story of Her earthly pilgrimage in time, this Marian Presence has been revealed to surround the Church like a mantle, like an 'added dimension', a climate, in which the 'seed of the Woman' would be nurtured and would prosper, and learn that they are the inheritors of the perpetual enmity as well as of its final victory...

St. Paul, in his second latter to the Thessalonians, reveals that 'something' is holding back 'the man of perdition', and that his listeners knew what it was. Since the Church in Her own Passion and crucifixion models Herself on Her beloved Spouse and Saviour, maybe we can learn from the circumstances of His Life what St. Paul meant, and what all this means for us.

No one could lay a hand on Christ as long as 'His hour' had not yet come. Nothing escapes Him. Everything is subject to His Authority. He decides, time, place and circumstances. 'His' hour had come when He instituted the Blessed Eucharist. After that, He told 'the seed of Satan': 'This is your hour'.

The Blessed Eucharist. The centre of everything!

'The Beast' will not come but on a signal of the Church, a 'sign', like the sign of the Blessed Eucharist. A decision that She too is prepared to lay down Her life for the salvation of the world. In total conformity with the Life and Death of Her Head. This will be 'Her finest hour'. After that, it will be the hour once again of the powers of darkness, the 'son of perdition': 'Satan's seed'.

No one can take the life of the Church. SHE ALONE can lay it down freely Herself. The decision has to come from Her. Has that decision been taken? Has She given the signal, the sign?

Maybe we should have a second look at the Documents of Vatican II ....

Why are the noisy modernists so confident, that their frivolous and casual acquaintance 'with the Documents of Vatican II', allows them to *identify* themselves with 'the world'? That is, to embrace the world *in a Teilhardian sense*? Have they once again 'perverted a given Revelation at its source'? If so, then they are truly part of 'the 200 million horsemen with serpent's tails'! *And so is their father Teilhard de Chardin*!

Maybe 'if this scroll is digested' if we ponder about these precious Documents of Vatican II, and meditate over them, we will discover the hard and *bitter* Truth of Vatican II: that we are asked by the Church 'to love the world' as *Christ did*! That is, embrace the world '*in a crucified sense* ...' We may discover that the Church, through these Documents, is preparing us for universal persecutions, and for that reason is trying to gather us *within the Marian Dimension as 'Mary's seed'*, not only for our protection, but also for the final victory over the forces of Evil. That would throw considerable more Light on the first part of Chapter Ten: the Marian teaching of the Supreme teaching Authority in the Church, 'Thunder' ...

And could it be, that the Marian Catholics have understood that message as no others, and are putting it already into practise ...?

Old Testament References in Chapter 10

Ezk 2:10. [p.1363]. (v.2)

See second reference in Chapter Five.

Am 3:8. [p.1480]. (v.3)

The lion roars: who can help feeling afraid?

The Lord Yahweh speaks: who can refuse to prophesy?

Ps 29:3-9. [p.810]. (v.3)

'Hymn to the Lord of the Storm'.

The tempest evokes the glory and the power of God [Ex 13:22 + and Ex 19:16 +], subduing the enemies of Israel and assuring peace to the Chosen People.

Jr 25:30. [p.1294]. (v.3)

"Yahweh roars from on high, He makes His voice heard from His holy dwelling place; He roars loud against His sheepfold, He shouts aloud like those who tread the grapes. The sound reaches all the inhabitants of the earth, to the far ends of the world.

FOR YAHWEH IS INDICTING THE NATIONS ... See, the disaster spreads from nation to nation."

Dn 8:26. [p.1440]. (v.4)

'This explanation of the mornings and evenings is true, but you must keep the vision secret, for there are still many days to go.'

Dn 12:4. [p.1446]. (v.4)

'But you, Daniel, must keep these words secret and the book sealed until the time of the End. Many will wander this way and that and wickedness will go on increasing.'

Dn 12:9. [p.1446]. (v.4)

'Daniel' he said, 'go away: these words are to remain secret and sealed UNTIL THE TIME OF THE END. Many will be cleansed, made white and purged; the wicked will go on doing wrong; the wicked will never understand; the learned will understand ...'

Dn 12:7. [p.1446]. (v.4)

'I heard the man speak who was dressed in linen, standing further up the stream: he raised his right hand to heaven and his left, and swore by Him who lives forever, "A time and two times, and half a time; and all these things are going to happen when he who crushes the power of the holy people meets his end".'

Dt 32:40. [p.259]. (v.5,6)

"Yes, I lift up my hand to heaven, and I say: 'As surely as I live forever, when I have whetted my flashing sword, I will take up the cause of right ...'"

Ne 9:6. [p.590]. (v.6)

Yahweh, you are the only one. You made the heavens, the heaven of heavens, with all their array, the earth and all it bears, the seas and all they hold. To all of these You give life and the array of heaven bows down before You.

Ex 20:11. [p.102]. (v.6)

For in six days Yahweh made the heavens and the earth and the sea and all they hold.

Ezk 12:28. [p.1372]. (v.7)

Very well, tell them, 'The Lord Yahweh says this: there will be no further delay in the fulfilling of any of My words. What I say is said and will come true – it is the Lord Yahweh who speaks.'

Am 3:7. [p.1480]. (v.7)

No more does the Lord Yahweh do anything without revealing His plans to His servants the prophets.

Zc 5:2. [p.1533]. (v.9-11)

The Angel who was talking to me said, 'What can you see?' I replied, 'I can see a flying scroll ...' He then said to me, 'This is the Curse sweeping across the face of the whole country ...'

Ezk 3:1-3. [p.1363]. (v.10)

He said, 'Son of man, eat this scroll ...' I ate it and it tasted sweet as honey.

Interlude: The Prayer of Daniel

In the first year of the reign of Darius I, Daniel was perusing the Scriptures, counting over the number of years – as revealed by Yahweh to the prophet Jeremiah – that were to pass before the successive devastations of Jerusalem would come to an end, namely seventy years. I turned my face to the Lord God begging for time to pray and to plead with fasting, sackcloth and ashes. I pleaded with Yahweh my God and made this confession:

"O Lord God, great and to be feared, You keep the Covenant and have kindness to those who love You and keep Your Commandments: we have sinned, we have done wrong, we have acted wickedly, we have betrayed Your Commandments and Your Ordinances and turned away from them. We have not listened to Your servants, the prophets who spoke in Your Name to our kings, our princes, our ancestors, and to all the people in the land. Integrity, Lord, is Yours, ours the look of shame we wear today, we, the people of Judah, the citizens of Jerusalem, the whole of Israel, near and far away, in every country to which You have dispersed us because of the treason we have committed against You. To the Lord our God mercy and pardon belong, because we have betrayed Him, and we have not listened to the voice of Yahweh our God, nor followed the laws He has given us through His servants the prophets. The whole of Israel has flouted Your law and turned away, unwilling to listen to Your voice; and the curse and imprecation written in the Law of Moses, the servant of God, have come pouring down on us – because we have sinned against Him. He has carried out the threats which He made against us and against the princes who governed us – that He would bring so great a disaster down on us that the fate of Jerusalem would find no parallel in the whole of the world. And now all this disaster has happened to us, just as it is written in the Law of Moses; even so, we have not tried to appease Yahweh by renouncing our crimes *and being guided by Your Truth.* Yahweh has watched for the right moment to bring disaster on us, since

> Yahweh our God is just in all His dealings with us, and we have not listened to His voice.
>
> And now Lord our God, who by Your mighty hand brought us out of the land of Egypt – the renown You won endures to this day – we have sinned, we have done wrong. Lord, by all Your acts of justice, turn away Your anger and your fury from Jerusalem, Your own city, Your holy mountain, for as a result of our sins and the crimes of our ancestors, Jerusalem and Your own people have become a byword among all around us. And now our God, listen to the prayer and the pleading of Your servant. For Your own sake, Lord, let Your face smile again *on Your desolate Sanctuary*. Listen my God, listen to us: open your eyes and look on our plight and on the city that bears Your Name. We are not relying on our own good works but on Your great mercy, to commend our humble plea to You. Listen, God, forgive! Hear, Lord, and act! For Your own sake, my God, do not delay, because they bear Your Name, this is Your city, this is your people!"

I was still speaking, still at prayer, confessing my own sins and the sins of my people Israel, and placing my plea before Yahweh my God for the holy mountain of my God, still speaking, still at prayer, when Gabriel, the being I had seen originally in a vision, flew suddenly down to me at the hour of the evening sacrifice. He said to me, 'Daniel, you see me; I have some down to teach you how to understand. When your pleading began, *a word was uttered* and I have come to tell you what it is ...' (Dn 9:2-23).

How strongly we are reminded here of 'another visitation by the Angel Gabriel', to Someone else in prayer, pleading with God, at the time of the evening Angelus ... And while She was at prayer, 'a word was not only uttered': "*The Word was made flesh* ..." and full understanding had at last made its home on our earth.

We too need to pray like this so that mercy and understanding may be given to us as well. Full understanding of the all-important role of our Heavenly Mother in the crucial days ahead ... And mercy, that our sins may not be in the way of the Light of Supernatural Understanding ...

Chapter Six

The Blessed Virgin Mary and the Final Confrontation Chapters Eleven and Twelve of the Apocalypse

A great climax is near at hand. The build-up towards it is powerful and compelling. Soon Satan will be forced to unmask and introduce his most potent 'seed', worse than 'the four evil spirits' he was allowed to release from 'the Euphrates'. The Champion on the side of God and the Church cannot be far away either.

Twenty-five centuries ago, Daniel had been shown the scene. He described the beast and its power and activities. But God's Champion remained a closely guarded secret, when he asked, "*My Lord, what is to be the outcome*?" Since, as we saw, Our Lord Himself introduced the Prophet Daniel in the very first chapter of the Book of Revelation, to impress on us that the visions received by His servant were still relevant and had not yet received their final, or even their most important, fulfillment in the Old Testament, here then once again is the biblical text of the final vision received by Daniel. For two most striking similarities it has immediate reference to the part of the Apocalypse where we are now.

> Then I, Daniel, looked on and saw two others standing, one on the near bank of the river, and one on the other. One said to the man dressed in linen who was standing further up the stream, 'how long till these wonders take place?' I

heard the man speak who was dressed in linen, standing further up the stream: *he raised his right hand and his left to heaven and swore by Him who lives forever*, 'A time and two times, and a half time; and all these things are going to happen when he who crushes the power of the holy people meets his end'. I listened but I did not understand. Then I said, '*My Lord, what is to be the outcome*?' 'Daniel', he said, 'go away: these words are to remain secret and sealed until the time of the End. Many will be cleansed, made white and purged; the wicked will go on doing wrong; the wicked will never understand; the learned will understand. From the moment the Perpetual Sacrifice is abolished and the disastrous abomination erected: one thousand two hundred and ninety days. Blessed is he who stands firm and attains a thousand three hundred and thirty five days. But you go away and rest; and you will rise for your share at the end of Time'. [Dn 12: 5-13].

Daniel's Prayer and its immediate aftermath are a vivid reminder of Our Lady's Annunciation by the same Archangel Gabriel, right at the beginning of the New Testament. This means that it was God's far-reaching Will, to have already a strong but concealed reference to Our Blessed Lady present in Daniel's visions, to be understood at a later date. But that is not the only reference to Our Lady.

The answer to Daniel's query: '*My Lord, what is to be the outcome*?' can now be supplied by any 'child of Mary': 'A great victory for the Church by a special intervention of Our Blessed Lady'. But

Daniel was not informed of this truth, but was told instead: 'these words (just spoken by that child), are to remain secret and sealed ...' God knows that the child spoke the truth. Which means that Our Lady, as the true answer to Daniel's question, was already present there and then in Daniel's time. But not yet in the rich detail as we know Her now.

By God's special design, the events narrated in this scene take us to the far end of the New Testament: to the previous chapter in the Book of Revelation, where another powerful Angel 'swears an oath to Him who lives forever' about the same beginning of the End, and where utterances related to the End 'are sealed and kept secret' until the time of their revelation has come. If, by the Will of God, Our Blessed Lady is already present in Daniel's visions and prophecies, how much more must Her presence be felt here in an identical scene in the Apocalypse, when the consoling news of Her complete manifestation is imminent?

Daniel then confirms our conclusion, drawn from evidence submitted and studied in the previous section: that at least part of what the 'Seven Thunders' said must have been in relation to Our Blessed Lady, which, translated, we recognise as the exercise of the highest teaching authority in the Church in defining the two great Marian Dogmas of the Immaculate Conception and Her glorious Assumption. It was God's idea to develop the Marian Dimension slowly and with infinite care and for the early Church it was not opportune to know the details of future highlights in advance with great precision. On the other hand it was necessary for the later manifestation to be able to point to *continuity* from early beginnings, which paradox was solved by God in the only way which, as we observed, does justice to both requirements:

(i) Our Lady is present in Daniel's prayer as well as in the unspoken answers to the question-marks in his vision 'on the time of the End'

(ii) Identical scenes and wordings relate Daniel to the tenth chapter of the Apocalypse, where it is no longer possible to conceal adequately the presence of Our Blessed Lady.

Fortified by this knowledge, we are now able to look for further developments of the existence of 'the Marian Dimension' in Chapter Eleven.

Section 11

The Sanctuary Measured
The Two Witnesses
The Ark of the Covenant Revealed
Chapter Eleven of the Apocalypse

I. Fr. Kramer's Commentary on the Measuring of the Sanctuary

The only other two instances in Scripture of 'measuring': the measuring of Jerusalem [Zc 2:1] and the measuring of the Temple [Ez 40:3] presaged *rebuilding*: the rebuilding of Jerusalem and of the Temple after the Babylonian Captivity. But no 'rod' was used in either case. In prophetic usage, the ROD is the symbol of the severity by which the faithful are separated from the unfaithful. [Zc 11:7]. It is the symbol of authority which is here of Divine origin and by Divine Right. Since everything except the Sanctuary is to be 'cast out', the separation by measuring signifies the preservation of the true believers in the severe ('rod') judgements to follow, because they are 'in the Sanctuary of God', they are 'sealed'. The seer is not to measure the city, nor the outer court, nor the whole Temple, but only the 'Sanctuary'. The 'rod' portents thus a decrease in the size of the Church, a restriction to 'the altar' and those who adore at the altar: the faithful bishops, priests and practising catholics who have the true worship and believe in the Eucharistic Presence. All who will not worship at the true altar, who do not adore the Eucharistic Christ, will in the crucial days ahead be in danger of submitting to the forces of Antichrist.

The measuring of the Sanctuary carries therefore the imitation of the zealous work on the part of the Hierarchy to teach and instruct, and the keenest eagerness on the part of the laity to become fully instructed in the Faith so as not to be deceived by the doctrines, the wonders and signs of 'the four evil spirits' still at large and operative in preparation for Antichrist. The searching test of Faith will leave in the Church only those who rather lose all than their Faith. Such faithfulness will be possible only for all who before this Day have lived the teachings of the Church, or join Her with full conviction and intention to sacrifice everything for It, and have been developed, enlightened and strengthened by Grace, especially Eucharistic Grace, through the frequent reception of the Body and Blood of Christ.

No one can be a member of the Church and a friend and follower of Antichrist. Since the forces of the latter are allowed to trample all over the outer court and the 'holy city', it means a definite division amongst the 'catholics'.

It is here that the Divine Strategy, gently but inexorably pursued through the whole of the Apocalypse, finally breaks through the surface to conclude the preparation for the full revelation in the next chapter. Here it becomes impossible to separate the Catholic Church from Our Lady, or Our Lady from the Catholic Church. Here the Dawn of a great understanding is breaking; here we see the reason why *the Morning Star* was given to those who persevered; why Christ wrote *His Mother's Name* on the pillars in God's Sanctuary, and why *non-deception* was irrevocably linked by St. Paul, under direct Divine Inspiration, with '*the New Eve*', in Tim. 2:14. Here we are back in the Sanctuary of the true Church; we are also back 'in God's Sanctuary: Mary'. Here we are talking about 'persevering Catholics', Catholics who are *not going to be deceived!* We are also referring to them as, or equating them with, '*Marian Catholics*'. Catholics, who have found 'the fruit of Her womb, Jesus', in frequent Communion. Catholics who, far from having found devotion to Our Blessed Lady an obstacle on their road to Christ, found it for them the quickest road to Him, since She is the 'Porta Coeli', the 'Door of Heaven' through which the Incarnation took place. Catholics, then, who took the teachings of the Church to their hearts and dared to see the Catholic Church as the Marian Church. And now Understanding, the Second Gift from the Holy Spirit, breaks forth as a new Dawn, that all this was meant by God, when in Paradise, he gave 'The Woman' the command to 'gather

Her seed', and fully instruct it in the essentials and strategies of 'that everlasting enmity' which they too were to inherit from Her. Over the centuries, only God has faithfully kept in mind his First Promise, His First Prophecy, and, like all things of God, it could not be thwarted, it could not fade.

And now we know Who will be the Champion on the side of God, and Whom God had in Mind when He spoke in Paradise to field against 'antichrist' Satan's main and final seed: the Virgin; the Church that contained 'the Blessed Eucharist', Her Son, and all those Marian Catholics who had no trouble seeing Her as the Mother and Model of the Church. God has but one 'Sanctuary'. Since He was Bodily present in the Blessed Virgin Mary, and is still Bodily present in the Blessed Eucharist in the *Catholic* Church, the imagery of 'the Sanctuary' must cover both. The 'outer court' and the 'holy city' must be all those catholics who have gone over to a modernistic, teilhardian interpretation of their Faith, which is absolutely incompatible with Our Blessed Lady and devotion to Her.

Fr. Kramer had great difficulty allocating other christians a place in this 'division', clearly marked to be 'severe'. This difficulty disappears when we take into account the great devotion to Our Blessed Lady which is awakening in all sorts of people of all sorts of denominations and persuasions. The Marian efforts of the true Church have found a fertile soil in many souls not immediately seen as being 'in communion with Rome'. When the days will grow steadily darker, who knows if 'the lighted candles in front of the Statue of Our Lady', i.e. the glowing devotion to the Mother of God by all faithful Catholics, 'shining out as a welcoming light', is not having an almost irresistible appeal 'on the other seed of the Woman' which She is to gather on the Father's Command from wherever She finds a response?

II. Fr. Kramer's Commentary on the Two Witnesses

Two places in the Old Testament relate to this vision in the Apocalypse

1. *Malachias 4:5*, where the prophet says: 'Behold, I will send you Elias, the prophet, before the coming of the great and dreadful Day of the Lord'.
2. *Zacharias 4:3, 14*; as quoted in the attached pages.

Because the original Greek has here the definite article, 'THE Two Witnesses ...', reference is made here to two definite personages, as in the quote from Zacharias, where reference is made to the high priest Joshua and the prince Zorobabel, i.e. two leaders, one civil, the other religious, who restored the Theocracy after the Babylonian Captivity.

Since a Martyr's Death is clearly foretold here by St. John for both Witnesses, it is obvious that neither of them can be anyone who has already died: nobody dies twice. Therefore Fr. Kramer accepts the Tradition which sees in these Two Personages HENOCH and ELIAS. Of both of them we have Scriptural evidence, that they were 'taken up', or 'translated', to be kept somewhere in readiness. (2 Ki 2:12; Hebr 11:5). Our Lord clearly predicted the coming of Elias: "Elias indeed shall come, and restore all things". (Mt 17:11; Mk 9:11).

'Restoring all things' is precisely the mandate received by the Two Witnesses, according to the description given here by St. John. And they will have power and authority to carry out their allotted task until their mission is accomplished. Already the Old Testament bears witness to the power of Elias to make fire come down from heaven on his command to destroy his adversaries, (2 Ki 1:10-13), and to order a drought of three and a half years duration, (2 Ki 17:1).

During the entire time of their appearance, the Two will testify by word and miracles to the Divine Origin of the Catholic Church alone, condemn all scandals within it, bear witness to the Divinity of Jesus Christ, and expose the imposture and blasphemy of the satanic forces of Antichrist. They appear to be very effective amongst the Jews, according to the biblical reference: 'Olive Trees', which is a sign of mercy. Many of them will reject Antichrist. The power of the Two Witnesses will also have largely undone the work of Antichrist elsewhere. All people who could have been converted shall have been converted: THE GOOD SHALL HAVE BEEN SEPARATED FROM THE WICKED, (the 'measuring of the Sanctuary'), and thus the work of the Prophets is complete.

'The Beast' is mentioned here for the first time. Various kinds of creatures have appeared heretofore, but no beast. The definite article: THE beast, used in this text, seems to presume some knowledge of this beast in the reader. The logical connection is to relate it to 'the beast' in the visions of Daniel, (which again means, that Daniel's prophecies have yet to be completely fulfilled, and that his visions have not yet fully come to pass. FA). Here, the beast ascends from the abyss, first mentioned in chapter nine, when it was opened by the 'fallen star', showing its satanic origin. In chapter thirteen, he rises up out of the 'sea', which means out of turmoil and revolutions. If we combine these two 'origins' we must assume that the human race became more and more drawn into Satan's principles and ethics, which began with the apostasy of the 'fallen star', received great impetus from the 'secret societies', the 'Euphrates', has been speeded up ever more on a global scale by Communism, Humanism and their allies under the world dominion of 'the beast'. Then the 'four evil spirits' will have finished their job, and will have fused with 'the beast', which means the end of the 'Second Woe'.

It is easily verifiable, that this chapter and the second one hereafter, chapter thirteen, both relate to events which take place during the reign of the beast. That way they become inseparable as two sides of the one coin. This side gives us the public appearance and global activities of the 'Two Witnesses', whereas chapter thirteen describes the activities of the beast, with God's Champion working behind the scenes. Since it is obvious that 'God's Champion' must be active in both scenes *since they cover one and the same period in time*, the big question is now very pertinent: '*Are these Two Witnesses MARIAN Saints*?' 'Is it Our Blessed Lady working with them for the glory of God and the Church?'

In the case of Elias, the ways of God are truly amazing. For Elias was so revered amongst the Essenes of Mount Carmel and Mount Horeb, *that he is considered by one of the oldest Marian Orders in the Church, the Carmelites, as their Founder*! If that does not place 'the roots of the Marian Dimension deep into the salvation history of the Old Testament', I do not know what would. And if that does not extend 'the same Marian Dimension' from the time of Elias right up to the time of Antichrist, nothing will. If one was to ask: 'Who in the Old Testament would closest resemble a Marian Religious of the Christian Era?', one would have to point to Elias. And if God were to ask us: "Whom shall I select, amongst all the people of the earth, to fight for the renewal of the Church at the height of the fulfillment of My Father's Prophecy in Paradise: 'the crushing of Satan's head by the Woman'?" would we, like God does here, overlook all the Christians of our own era, future Saints amongst them, and point to Elias from the Old Regime as the most suitable instrument in His Hand? ... Would we? Such honour for the Old Testament! And what an indictment it is on the softness and timidity of us, Western catholics of our own era who, in the face of the monstrous Modernism of our days, seem to have forgotten what it means to belong to *the Church Militant* ...

With this so beautifully arranged by God, we may now extend the vision, and soberly see in the struggle of the Two Witnesses, the fight-to-the-death of every Marian soldier in those days, inspired by the heroic work of Elias and Henoch. And that it is none too soon, we can learn from the following words:

> 'In those days, Faith will have sunk very low, and it will be preserved in some places only, and in a few cottages and in a few families which God has protected from disasters and wars.' [Ven. Anna Catharina Emmerich]

Catholics who have nurtured a great devotion to Our Blessed Lady to preserve their own Faith and that of the ones entrusted to their care: all those, in other words, found worthy 'to be measured inside the Sanctuary', will be given the opportunity and grace, to proclaim that Faith fearlessly in the open once again, and to resist, with all the Supernatural Might that this places at their disposal, the final onslaught of Evil 'on the Sanctuary'. And then, and only then, will Modernism, Humanism, Communism and Evolution *be cast out of the Church: chapter twelve*, and make way for the Invincible Power of the Cross, marking the end of 'the Second Woe'. These Marian Catholics had to suffer under the 'four evil spirits' and under the Beast, but they no longer have to fear 'the Third Woe', for that is inflicted only on the followers of the Beast.

III. Fr. Kramer's Commentary on the 'Seventh Trumpet'

The Third Woe will descend directly on the followers of the Beast. This Woe will begin in Chapter Sixteen. The activity and success of the Beast and the False Prophet must first be staged after the judgement upon the Church and Her conflict with Satan has been described, Chapters Twelve – Fourteen.

The Seventh Trumpet is instantly answered by jubilant voices from 'heaven'. These voices anticipate the victory still in the future. Like Jeremias, (50:2), announced 'the fall of Babylon' as if it were already a past event. The voices are 'in the Church', starting with the powerful voices of the four living beings, the Episcopate *in its unity with the Pope and the Lamb*, followed by the Priesthood, represented by the twenty-four Elders. Those who speak know the signs, admonish and instruct the people and confirm them in the expectation of a great and speedy victory. They are 'great voices': a teaching that will be heard far and wide and given with authority, and so trusted by the faithful. (Jer. 25: 30-31).

Although the victory is announced in advance with positive certainty, those who raise their voices are still threatened with death at the hands of Antichrist and his followers. But forgetting their own peril, they rejoice in the victory of Christ and His Church. They know that Christ's universal Kingdom will now become a reality, that it will never end, *and that all promises made through the Prophets shall be fulfilled.* The new establishment of the Old Church will prove for all times that no power on earth can destroy it. The words '*our Lord and His Christ*' are taken from Psalm 2: 2. The same exultation is expressed in Chapter 12: 10, and Chapter 19: 6. God will now convert all nations and rule forever. St. John here makes the whole of Psalm 2 a prophecy pointing to Antichrist and his followers and it should be read in the light. The nations subject to his tyranny were angry with God, which is a most unnatural and blasphemous attitude for a creature to assume towards its Creator. It is satanic. They raged against Him, fought against Him, blinded in their fury by the '*four evil spirits released from the Euphrates, polluted at its source*'. They even denied His existence; passed legislation to outlaw Him, His Goodness and His Mercy; and to oppress all who adore Him. His wrathful visitations were therefore made inevitable. These last plagues, which begin in Chapter Sixteen, would be averted if the wicked were converted by the Two Witnesses. They refused and hence their doom is now sealed.

The last verse, v. 19, is co-incident in time with Chapter 15: 5, and points to the end of Chapter 19. It is meant, therefore, to be a glimpse of the final judgement on the wicked, stating in an abbreviated form the 'Third Woe'. That Woe will have its fulfillment in Chapters 16 through to 19. Of the intervening Chapters, Chapter 12 depicts the Battle of the Church with Satan, and Chapter 13 with the two beasts, (as Chapter 11 described the combat between the beast and the Two Witnesses).

Chapter 14 describes the magnificent state of those who have kept themselves undefiled from the world of the beast, and Chapter 15 the blessed state of those who have conquered the beast and its evil: a laity full of the 'fire of God', deserving that, at last, their oppressors and tormentors be punished. These two chapters are obviously included for the encouragement of those who, under the tyranny of the beast and resisting its evil, experienced the ominous words of 13:7, already predicted by Daniel (Dn. 7: 21, 24, 25): "And it was given to it to make war with the saints *and to conquer them* ..."

The 'sanctuary of God' is again in view and is opened. This is only a momentary flash revealing the extraordinary divine power of the Church. God's judgement upon the world shall proceed from the inner sanctuary after the Church has Herself been judged and purified. The 'Ark of the Covenant' was lost, and the temple in the days of Our Lord did not contain it. Neither did Ezekiel see the Ark in the ideal temple. The 'ark of the Covenant' in the new 'sanctuary of God' is the 'place of rest' in His Church, the tabernacle where Christ dwells in the Blessed Eucharist. This reveals whence will come the power to execute judgement upon the world. The lightnings, voices, thunder-peals, earthquakes and hail are symbols of judgement.

Verse 19 is therefore not an introduction to Chapter 12, but a statement of the theme of Chapters 14-19 incl. It also puts the full close to Chapter 11, sums up the main events of the Seventh Trumpet and flashes forth a momentary glimpse of the final judgement upon the wicked. (End of, in the main, Fr. Kramer's commentary.)

The last paragraph quoted above, taken verbatim from Fr. Kramer's book, clearly shows up the inconsistencies with which an author is forced to put up, if a certain part of the Truth, of Reality, escapes him. No line in a continuous and highly organised Drama puts 'paid' to what went before in the middle of the action. Nowhere else in his Commentary would Fr. Kramer maintain that one chapter in the Apocalypse 'puts a full close' to the one directly preceding it. No part in the Apocalypse 'skips two chapters' just to find its continuation further on. In fact, even in spite of his declaration here, verse 19 is most certainly in Fr. Kramer's own mind an Introduction to Chapter 12. I have quoted his words '... *after the Church has Herself been judged and purified.*' That is part of his Commentary of Chapter 11. In the next chapter he rightly maintains that the 'throwing out of the Dragon from heaven' is the casting out of the devilish influence from the Church. This shows that, even to Fr. Kramer, there really is an unbroken line from Chapter 10 running right through Chapters 11 and 12, and beyond, which, after some study, will become obvious to anyone else as well.

God's first love is for His Daughter, His embattled Church. Christ's Love is for His Body, His beloved Bride, who finally, in Her own overflowing love for Him, now too is paying the highest price for fidelity to God's Will, and finds Herself on Her own road to Calvary, to be crucified for a human race, once again in the grip of the most diabolical forces, because, like God's city, Jerusalem, 'it too had not understood the moment of God's visitation and the hour of its deliverance'. The 'four evil spirits' have forced their way '*into Her heart and veins*' (Pascendi). Of the 200 million horsemen, some, the Communists, are persecuting Her children in a most terrible way. Others, the Marxist 'catholics', the Modernists, the Teilhardian Evolutionists and the Humanists, refuse to leave Her innermost Sanctuary and are choking Her and Her children almost to death with their poisonous doctrines. In Her dire affliction She is, as we shall soon see, crying out to God for Mercy and strength. And this is the hour set aside by God and kept in readiness after all those centuries for this very purpose: to reveal the One with Whom at last the Church is worthy to be identified, now that She too has accepted the crucifixion of Her own children. The One whom He has appointed 'to be Her Mother *and Her Model*!' The same One He had appointed in Paradise: 'to crush the serpent's head ...'

With this in mind, we may have a fresh look at the text of this chapter, to see what it reveals to us from this new angle.

Just as Elias, as we saw, is to be considered a Marian Saint of the Old Regime, kept in readiness to be revealed at the appropriate time, to fulfill a very special role in the Church, so also the 'Ark of the Covenant' (as the Litany of Loreto teaches us) is to be considered an Old Testament reference to Our Blessed Lady. At one time hidden by Jeremias (quote attached), it too is kept in readiness to be revealed by God 'at the appropriate time', to announce a very special role by Our Blessed Lady. So far, the 'little Lamb' has been used by St. John to refer to Christ in the Blessed Eucharist and to

His absolute power over world events to guide them to the service of His own ends. This role is now all of a sudden being taken over by the 'Ark of the Covenant' as Fr. Kramer will have us believe. The revelation of the Ark of the Covenant inside the Sanctuary of the Church is clearly preserved for this moment, not to take over the function and role of the 'little Lamb', but for its own function as ordained by God directly related to the work of Our Blessed Lady.

> The tremendous jubilation and relief of the whole Church expressed in the final part of this chapter is due to the fact that the Church has understood the *meaning* and the *timing* of this Divine Decree, and that Our Lady is recognized by the faithful as identifying Herself in a very special way with the Church to assist Her in Her final battle with Satan and his Antichrist.

What we hoped and believed and prayed over in the last chapter: that part of the explanation of the 'Seven Thunders' would be the declaration of some important Marian teaching within the Church, that we now know for certain did take place: to the great consolation of the Faithful, a very special presence of Our Blessed Lady within the Sanctuary of the Church has been revealed, not only through the Declaration of two Great Marian Dogmas, but also through the magnificent Mariology of the whole Church 'in council': the Second Vatican Council. Of this Council, a non-Catholic observer has remarked:

> "Strange as it may seem, this is the first full-orbed *conciliar* exposition of the doctrine of the Church in Christian history. Earlier Councils took the Church for granted and focused their energies on one or another challenge to her teaching or unity. Vatican II however, was an unprecedented venture in ecclesiological self-examination and self-understanding. Its working premise was the conviction *that any significant renovation of the Church-in-action* would have to begin with a valid doctrinal statement concerning her basic nature. Thus, the Constitution on the Church, '*Lumen Gentium*', is important both in its own right and also as the fundamentum of the other fifteen Documents of the Second Vatican Council." (Dr. Albert C. Outler in The Documents of Vatican II, W.M. Abbott, S.J., p.102).

Because of this, the post-Conciliar modernists are in a deep quandary, for the Holy Spirit prevented the Council Fathers from issuing a separate Document on Our Lady, and instead, through the celebrated Council decision of dealing with Our Blessed Lady in this Dogmatic Constitution of the Church, *He made the Mother of God inseparable from the Church*!

In fact, the Teilhardian and Marxist representatives of 'the four evil spirits' within the Church are in an impossible position, for the Holy Spirit went even further than that, and made the Council revive the ancient Catholic doctrine '*that Our Lady is the Proto-Type of the Church*'. Which means that any attempts the Modernists make to separate the Blessed Virgin Mary from any 'church' they envisage, automatically classify such a 'church' as *non-catholic* and not the one envisaged by Vatican II.

And to add even further to their acute discomfort, the Second Vatican Council bases the Introduction to its deliberations on Our Lady on one text, and one text only, a famous text by *St. Iraeneus* of the second century, a disciple of *St. Polycarp*, who in turn listened to the preaching of the *Apostle St. John*, the one who put 'the Marian Dimension' within the Apocalypse .... This text of St. Irenaeus has set the tone *for the whole Tradition in the Catholic Church on Our Lady*, and in quoting this text, evoking all the surrounding doctrine it entails, Vatican II did not only base its own deliberations on Our Lady squarely on Tradition, but in going back as far as she possibly could, the Council made her teaching akin to infallible teaching without having to define it as such. The riches in vision and depth of the teaching on Our Lady that follow then are majestic and a truly magnificent and fitting setting for a Church which, fully aware of the gravity of the moment, and in the full knowledge 'that Her own hour at last had come', in preparing Herself for a momentous decision which She did not want to take and execute in isolation, but under the steadfast protection of Her, whom She in Her hour of greatest need graced with the name and title of '*Mary, Mother and Model of the Church*'.

With this teaching, Mary has been revealed as belonging to the essence, to the nature of the Church. That is, She, 'the Ark of the Covenant', has been revealed to be *within the Sanctuary of the Church*! And from this position, MARY IS PRESENT at every 'sermon', at every 'seminary lecture', at every 'catechetics class' and at every 'seminar' where a marxist priest, a modernist 'theologian', a teilhardian 'nun' or any other humanistic representative of 'the 200 million horsemen' *tries to deceive 'Her seed'*, tries to remove from the hands of the little ones, entrusted to Her by the Father, *the Morning Star*, tries to rub out Her Name *from the pillars in the Sanctuary of Her God ...*

And it is also from this position that She will begin the execution of the mandate entrusted to Her by the Father from the beginning: to perpetuate the eternal enmity between Satan's seed and Hers, and to finally crush his infernal head ... This means first of all, as we will see in the continuation of the Divine Drama in the next chapter: the cleaning out of the Sanctuary with the 'great hail' that accompanied the manifestation of the Ark of the Covenant within the Sanctuary.

Old Testament References in Chapter 11

Ezk 40:1-5. [p. 1410]. (v.1)

"In the twenty-fifth year of our captivity, at the beginning of the year, on the tenth day of the month, fourteen years after the destruction of the city [Sep-Oct 573], the hand of Yahweh came on me."

[One of the most solemn openings of any chapter in Sacred Scripture, akin to the one preceding the public ministry of John the Baptist; it must introduce a most important event.]

"In a divine vision He took me away to the land of Israel and put me down on a very high mountain on the south of which there seemed to be built a city. He took me to it and there I saw a man who seemed to be made of bronze. He had a flax cord and a measuring rod in his hand and was standing in the gateway. The man said to me, 'Son of man, look carefully, listen closely and pay attention to everything I show you, since you have only been brought here for me to show it to you. Tell the house of Israel everything that you see.'

The temple was surrounded with a wall, and the man was holding a measuring rod six cubits long, each cubit a forearm and a hand's breadth. He measured the thickness of the construction – one rod; and its height – one rod.

He went to the east gate ..."

Zc 2:5-9. [p.1531]. (v.1)

Then, raising my eyes, I saw a vision. It was this: there was a man with a measuring line in his hand. I asked him 'Where are you going?' He said, 'To measure Jerusalem, to find out her breadth and her length.' And then, when the Angel who was talking to me stood still, another Angel came forward to meet him. He said to him, 'Run, and tell the young man this: "Jerusalem is to remain unwalled because of the great number of men and cattle there will be in her. But I – it is Yahweh who speaks – I will be a wall of fire for her all round her, and I will be her glory in the midst of her".'

Dn 7:25. [p.1438]. (v.3)

' ... he is going to speak words against the Most High
and harass the Saints of the most High,
He will consider changing seasons and the Law,
and the Saints will be put into his power
for a time, two times, and a half time ...'

Zc 4:3, 14. [p.1532]. (v.4)

By it are two olive trees, one to the right of it and one to the left. Speaking again, I said to the Angel who was talking to me, 'What do these things mean, my lord?' He said, 'These are the two anointed ones who stand before the Lord of the whole world'.

2K 1:10. [p.454]. (v.5)

Elijah answered the captain, 'If I am a man of God, let fire come down from heaven and destroy both you and your fifty men'. And fire came down from heaven and destroyed him and his fifty men.

Jr 5:14. [p.1259]. (v.5)

'Now I will make My words
a fire in your mouth,
and make this people wood
for the fire to devour'.

1K 17:1. [p.443]. (v.6)

Elijah the Tishbite, of Tishbe in Gilead, said to Ahab, 'As Yahweh lives, the God of Israel whom I serve, there shall be neither dew nor rain these years except at my order'.

Ex 1:17. [p.86]. (v.6)

Here is Yahweh's message, That I am Yahweh you shall learn by this: with the staff that is in my hand I will strike the water of the river and it shall be changed into blood.'

Dn 7:21. [p.1438]. (v.7)

This was the horn I had watched making war on the saints and proving stronger, until the coming of the One of great age who gave judgement in favour of the saints of the Most High, when the time came for the saints to take over the Kingdom.

Est 9:19. [p.652]. (v.10)

This is why Jewish country people, those who live in undefended villages, keep the fourteenth day of the month of Adar as a day of gladness, feasting and holiday-making, and exchange presents with one another.

Ezk 37:5,10. [p.1407]. (v.11)

5. The Lord Yahweh says this to these bones: I am now going to make the breath enter you, and you will live.

10. I prophesied as He had ordered me and the breath entered them; they came to life again and stood up on their feet, a great, an immense army.

2K 2:11. [p.455]. (v.12)

Now as they walked on, talking as they went, a chariot of fire appeared and horses of fire, coming between the two of them; and Elijah went up to heaven in the whirlwind. Elisha saw it and cried: 'My father! My father! Chariot of Israel and its chargers!'

Ezk 7:5. [p.1367]. (v.14)

The Lord Yahweh says this: now disaster is going to follow on disaster ... Now it is your turn, you who live in the country ...

Ps 2. [p.786]. (v.15)

[The horizon of this short Psalm is the future Messianic age. Although all of it is applicable here, some verses stand out:]

8. Ask and I will give You the nations for your heritage,
the ends of the earth for Your domain.

[Another verse will be quoted a bit further on.]

Ps 22:28. [p.804]. (v.15)

For Yahweh reigns, the Ruler of the Nations!
Before Him all the prosperous of the earth will bow down.

Dn 7:14. [p.1437].

On Him [i.e. one like a Son of Man] was conferred sovereignty, glory and kingship,
and men of all peoples, nations and languages became His servants.

Dn 7:27. [p.1438]. (v.15)

And the sovereignty and kingship,
and the splendors of all the kingdoms under heaven
will be given to the people of the saints of the Most High.
His sovereignty is an eternal sovereignty
and every empire will serve and obey Him.

Zc 14:9. [p.1542]. (v.15)

And Yahweh will be King of the whole world. When that day comes, Yahweh will be unique and His Name unique.

Ps 2:1,5. [p.786]. (v.18)

1. Why this uproar among the nations?
Why this impotent rage of the pagans –
kings on earth rising in revolt,
princes plotting against Yahweh and His Anointed?
5. Then, in a rage, He strikes them with panic.

Am 3:7. [p.1480]. (v.18)

No more does the Lord Yahweh do anything
without revealing His plans to His servants the prophets.

Ps 115:13. [p.900]. (v.18)

He will bless those who fear Yahweh

without distinction or rank.

Ex 25:8-10+ [p.108]. (v.19)

'Build Me a sanctuary so that I may dwell among them. In making the Tabernacle and its furnishings you must follow the pattern I shall show you.'

2M 2:5-8. [p.695. (v.19)

On his arrival (on Mt. Nebo, where Moses had died) Jeremiah found a cave-dwelling into which he brought the Tabernacle, the Ark, and the altar of incense, afterwards blocking up the entrance. Some of his companions came up to mark out the way, but were unable to find it. When Jeremiah learned this he reproached them: 'This place is to remain unknown', he said, '*until God gathers His people together again* and shows them His Mercy. Then the Lord will bring these things once more to light, and the glory of the Lord will be seen, and so will be the Cloud, as it was revealed in the time of Moses, and when Solomon prayed that the Holy Place might be gloriously hallowed'.

Section 12

The Great Apparitions of Our Lady
Their Consequences for the Church
Chapter Twelve of the Apocalypse

"And a great sign was seen in heaven: a Woman clothed with the sun, the moon under Her feet and upon Her head a crown of twelve stars."

There is not a Christian alive or dead, who, on reading those words, did not immediately think of Our Lady, and (since the middle of the nineteenth century), more specifically of Our Lady of Lourdes. And that is obviously the intention of the Author of these words, the Holy Spirit. Fr. Kramer, in categorically stating: 'The Woman of Chapter 12 is not the Blessed Virgin Mary', has placed himself in an untenable position, advancing an inadmissible theory that the Holy Spirit is playing tricks on people who naturally think that She is. Commentators who only see the Church represented by this Woman cannot, for support of their stand, point out that Our Lady was never in labour giving birth to Our Divine Saviour Jesus Christ, as His Birth was miraculous.

True. But Our Blessed Lady is not only Mother of the Head of the Church, and people who, for the above reasons, dismiss the 'sign' as representing Our Lady, entirely miss the point made here by God. For, in consenting to give birth to the Church, Our Lady *did* suffer grievously, and whilst She gave her 'second Fiat' on Calvary: 'to become also the Mother of the *members* of the Mystical Body of Christ', Mary *did* cry ... We may not dismiss Our Blessed Lady from this magnificent vision simply because the Woman cried 'giving birth'.

The reason why Fr. Kramer cannot see Our Lady *and* the Church portrayed here together in the *one* image is, because the whole gradual preparation for this fusion, woven into the Apocalypse as 'the Marian Dimension', escaped him altogether as we saw. But the unity between the Blessed Virgin and the Bride of the Lamb of God has always been there right from the beginning. That spiritual union between *model* and *faithful replica* is nothing forced or artificial: God placed it there from the beginning to be discovered and enjoyed. Those who did, have no trouble seeing here portrayed in the Woman, crying in giving birth, an image of our heavenly Mother, as the Mother of Seven Dolours, as well as of our Holy Mother the Catholic Church at the time of the great, universal and cruel persecutions under Antichrist. To be identified, then, at that time, with a Mother who understands suffering, and who knows the pains sustained in giving spiritual birth to sinners, must be very consoling to the whole Church. Tremendous gratitude is due to God for what He Himself started in Paradise, and kept alive during the Old Testament in the living Saints of that time. Gratitude for something, that was freely accepted and agreed upon 'as a second Fiat' on Calvary, only to be led, from then on, to its final fulfillment and glorious manifestation by the One Who guides everything according to the Will of His Father: the 'little Lamb', Christ our Lord in the Blessed Eucharist.

We have waited a long time for this. We have come a long way. During our journey through the Church's pilgrimage, the Blue Light of the Marian Dimension within the Church grew steadily brighter and stronger as the darkness which always surrounds Evil gradually spread once again through the whole human race. The teaching authority of the Church revealed the presence of the Mother of God right within the Sanctuary of the Church. Could anything else be done to make the Marian Dimension even more manifest? To vindicate completely the Truth of what God had set in motion after the Fall?

Our Blessed Lady Herself has given us the answers to these questions. SHE APPEARED .... That was all that was still possible to be done. 'A great sign appeared in the Church', and in two spectacular Apparitions the Virgin Mary confirmed everything the Church's teaching authority had revealed to us for our consolation. In 1858, Our Lady appeared to St. Bernadette near the obscure French village of Lourdes, to confirm the Dogma of the Immaculate Conception, promulgated four years earlier in 1854. And in 1917, Our Lady once again appeared, this time to three little children near the Portuguese village of Fatima, to reveal to the whole Church that it is God's Will, that His victory over evil would be Her victory, with these words: 'God wishes to establish on earth the devotion to My Immaculate Heart ..., for in the end, *My Immaculate Heart will triumph* ...' In other words, it is God's wish that She, together with all the ones 'who love Her Immaculate Heart' will finally crush Satan's head. The complete identification of the Mother and the children, the Mother and the Church, the Woman and Her Seed ... St. Jerome was right in translating the famous text of the First Prophecy in Latin as 'et IPSA conteret caput tuum ...': 'and SHE shall crush your head ...'. And the Church has been proven right in making this translation Her own. For Our Lady came down to confirm it: 'In the end My Immaculate Heart will triumph ...' Triumph over all evil, over all resistance, over all obstacles, over every opposition. It is God's Decree. And it is Her Son, 'Her First Seed', Her and our Saviour, Who, from the Sanctuary of His Church, has directed all world events to the fulfillment of His Father's Decree. He won the overall victory on the Cross, but He wishes to share it with His Mother, 'the New Eve'. And with Her other Children to whom She 'gave birth' through the Bride of the Lamb of God, Our Holy Mother the Catholic Church.

Now everything that God could possibly have done, has been done. The 'Marian Dimension' has been discretely foretold to exist, openly taught to exist, and now finally shown to exist. From now on we can safely trust the Church that possess this hallmark of Perfection, this stamp of Divine favour, *and mistrust any 'church' that is without it*! That this is a stipulation of the truly Infinite Wisdom of God which has the most far-reaching consequences, we will find out in the next chapter, and we will have to wait till then to give it all the glory and thanksgiving it deserves. First, a look at the other remarkable events in this highly dramatic Chapter 12.

> 'And another sign was seen in heaven, behold a great red dragon, *having seven heads and ten horns*, and upon his head seven diadems...'

We could contrast this with a sentence from the next chapter.

> 'And I beheld rising out of the sea a beast *which had ten horns and seven heads*, and upon its horns ten diadems ...'

Identical images used to describe these two appearances. We do not need much imagination to see where the beast gets 'his power and authority from', or for what purpose it appears in this world.

Satan rules (diadems) through his seven heads, whereas 'his seed' rules through its ten horns. The 'seven heads' of Satan would then most likely be 'the Seven Deadly Sins' by which he holds sway over peoples and nations. It would mean then, that, for Satan it is more important that people have allegiance to 'committing sin' and 'going to hell', rather than show allegiance to 'ten rulers' (political leaders) working under Satan; whereas 'the beast' must make sure that the 'ten leaders' appointed by him to do Satan's work are committed to him personally.

The tail of the dragon draws in its coils one third of the stars of Heaven and casts them to the earth. *This is one-third of the clergy.* 'Heaven' as we know is the 'Church', whereas 'the earth' is the profane, secular society outside Her. In Arianism, (6:13), there was great apostasy of bishops and priests. The stars fell from heaven, like figs in a storm. In the Greek Schism, a great star, the Patriarch, fell from heaven, (8:10); and a star fell from heaven who led the apostasy from the Church into the Reformation, (9:11). Before the appearance of Antichrist, then, *one-third of the bishops and priests shall follow the dragon* ... It is worthy of note that this second great sign also appeared 'in heaven', meaning Satan's influence in the Church through the pernicious evil of *Modernism, one of his 'four evil spirits',* which obviously accounts for the mass defection. The tail is the symbol of lying and hypocrisy. It seems to refer to Isaias, 9:15-16:

> Yahweh has cut head and tail from Israel: the 'head' is the elder and the man of rank, the 'tail' the prophet of lying visions.

So the adherence to heresies, and the subsequent apostasy from the Church, are mainly due to deception and deceit, against which the clergy did not guard themselves sufficiently with prayer, fasting, obedience to the Magisterium and *fervent devotion to the Mother of God* ...

We would be well advised, in the light of the gravity of the Revelations made here, to reread the 'Seven Letters' dictated by Christ to Seven Bishops in Asia Minor in chapters two and three, to see for ourselves to what sins amd bad habits the Divine Author takes exception as having the most terrible consequences, leading, if unchecked, to all sorts of other sins and irregularities. Mentioned are: a state of tepidity, loss of zeal and charity, and a decline of the spirit of penance and sacrifice.

Fr. Kramer lists here a number of Old Testament places, where the prophets warn against vices, mainly in the shepherds of the people, leading to apostasy from Yahweh and from communion with Him. Here are some of them:

Malachias	1:7,8,12	Isaias	30:10	Jeremias	23:2,11-17
	2:7,9,17		1:11-15		25:29
Daniel	11:32		56:2-3		5:31
Amos	5:10,12		23:5,7	Ezechiel	3:18-21
					34:2-6

'The male child' the Woman gives birth to under such adverse conditions, according to Fr. Kramer, is a Pope who will bring in the necessary reforms within the Church 'to end the influence of Satan'. A *Marian Pope*, since, as we saw, from now on 'the Woman' represents both the Church and Our Lady, working together quite openly for the good of the Church and the salvation of the world.

The 'rod of iron' refers to v.1 in the previous chapter: the measuring of the Sanctuary with a reed like unto a rod, symbol of Divine chastisement, or law-enforcement, separating the good from the wicked. *The Church will be purified*! The good will accept the enforcement of Divine Law and Church discipline, the wicked will rebel and apostasise. The words also refer to Psalm 2:9.

With this chapter we are on the borderline of what has come to pass and what has still to come. We recognise some of the symbols, and we may follow the general outline. But details, such as 'and the child was taken up to God and to His throne', could mean a variety of things. Early dedication to the service of God in the Church is one possibility. [We remember that in the Apocalypse 'God's throne' is in the middle of the Church: ch. 4, v.2]. Or a martyr's death after the purification of the Church, after which 'the Woman' is looked after by God 'in the wilderness'; etc. Since these *facts* are still somewhat in the future, (although their preparation, and the trends leading up to them, are clearly with us), their meaning is open to conjecture and speculation for which there is no room here. The length of time that the Church is looked after 'in the wilderness' coincides with the length of time during the public appearance of 'the Two Witnesses', and also with the time-span repeatedly mentioned by Daniel for the reign of the beast and the abolition of the Perpetual Sacrifice.

'The battle in heaven' is the fight between the faithful Catholics, headed by the Marian Pope 'with the rod of iron', and the Modernists. Since the presence of Our Lady 'within the Sanctuary' has been made manifest, the public appearance of the Majestic Lady spells the end of the 'occupation of the Sanctuary' by the Modernists and other minions of the 'four evil spirits'. Their allegiance is with the world, 'the earth', ("Building the Earth" is one of the books of their master-mind, Teilhard de Chardin!) and that is where they end up. This battle into which Michael enters with his might was announced *under oath* in chapter 10 v.5. The Judgement was to begin 'at the House of God' (1 Peter 4:17) and that is where it now starts. Individual bishops are referred to in the Apocalypse as 'stars' or 'angels'. "Write to the angel of the Church of ..." were the very words of Christ in chapters 2 and 3. The angels who fight under the leadership of 'Michael' are the loyal bishops and priests in the Church, while the angels of the dragon are the sinful priests and bishops, disloyal to the Church, the Holy Father and the Magisterium. They are at least one-third of the total number. Perhaps the appearance of the Two Witnesses will coincide with this battle, will precipitate things and polarise the two feuding camps more speedily.

The jubilation of the good after winning the battle is understandable. The term 'accuser of our brethren' comes from Job, 1:6 and 2:1. 'Accuser' refers to Satan's boasted success within the Church. He led many of the clergy to accept his doctrines, the maxims of the world, and through their compliance crowded out grace and the spirit of sacrifice and penance, with the consequent state of hypocrisy, lying, deceit, tepidity, immorality and finally spiritual death: all the very things Christ took serious issue with in His celebrated letters at the beginning. Since almost all the 'seminaries' the world over were hotbeds of this perversion, the brilliance of victory will be most markedly apparent in the whole area of Priestly formation, and the hatred of the defeat will become most violent and vitriolic in the resistance to the sanctification of the seminaries. Good priests come from holy seminaries, and holy seminaries are found 'in the Sanctuary of the Marian Dimension'...

Satan is now forced to attack the Church from without. His expulsion from the Sanctuary is described as a casting down on earth. This represents the Church as a Supernatural Institution in contrast to 'the world', which Satan will now plunge into vice as deeply as he can, to marshall the inhabitants of the world for his final attack on the Church. No longer capable of destroying the faithful members by deceit, he can now only turn to the violent means of persecutions.

As said before, we seem to find our times in the middle of events described here in the Apocalypse, which means we are not distant enough to get a complete understanding of the realities revealed to us in symbolism. That is no news to God, Who wrote the Book. So He knows that we cannot understand everything. He knows that we do not have to know everything. But He also knows that we can make an intelligent use of the past to get a good grip on the present. And He also knows that, if we neglect to do that, then the lack of understanding will be our own fault.

What, then, are some of the facts that have emerged so far, from which we can learn, and which, if taken into account, will secure us God's help, and a safe passage for ourselves as well as for the Church through the most terrible time of man's history?

1. Christ directs everything, to serve His Father's Will with the Elect, *from the Blessed Eucharist*. Nothing escapes Him; nothing can thwart His Will, not even the havoc caused by Sin, yes, not even the complete dislocation, caused by the 200 million humanists, communists, marxists and modernists. This means that all who want to serve Him and do His Holy Will *can live in Hope*: no detail in their lives is too small, too insignificant, not to have been

foreseen by Him and used by Him for His ends and their own salvation. Wickedness causes harm, untold harm, but even that is forced to serve God's ends with His Elect, His precious Church and Her work of Salvation...

If then we read in v.11: "And they have conquered him *through the Blood of the Lamb*", then we know that, what is meant here, is '*frequent Communion*'! We are not talking here of Martyrs: we have learned and come to appreciate that nowhere does the Apocalypse talk about the dead (except in one short sentence). Nothing is revealed about the Life hereafter. Right up to the end, 'heaven' is the Church! We are constantly dealing with the living. But that does not mean that their state of happiness in the service of God *here on earth* is not meant to be a *true* foretaste of their eternal happiness in the 'real' heaven. That's why the word 'heaven' for the 'Church' is carefully chosen by the Authors: God and St. John.

2. A second major revelation which has come to light so far, meant for a better understanding of our own times as well as for our future wellbeing, is the final identification of the Catholic Church with Our Blessed Lady. We have seen the long preparation, and we appreciate that the timing for the fullest revelation of this great unity, fixed by God from all eternity to coincide with our days, *is God's precious gift for the consolation and strength of the Christians, asked by Him to take themselves and the Church through the most terrible time of Antichrist.*

If, then, we read in v.17 the by now familiar and oft quoted words: "*to make war on the rest of Her seed ...*", we know that God has a very special reason for putting, in the Last Book of the Bible, His exact words which were written in the beginning of the First

Book of the Bible. For these words have a 'rider'. The First Book foretold the End: "*and She shall crush your head!*" So anyone who wants to come out on top, "now that the war has been declared", will have to stay with the One to whom the victory was promised. And if this victorious Woman is identified with a particular Church, then we do well to remain with that Church at all cost. For that Church too will be victorious. This means that '*frequent reception of the Eucharistic Lamb' in Holy Communion* will make of us '*Marian Catholics*'.

3. Finally, what happens to the '*Model*' happens to the '*replica*'. Since Our Blessed Lady and the Church founded by Christ have now been 'locked' under the same image of 'the Woman', what happens to 'this Woman' somehow happens to both Our Blessed Lady and the Church of which She is the Mother and Model.

In the final part of this chapter 12, St. John describes several things that happen to 'the Woman':

(a) ' ... he pursued the Woman ...'
(b) '... that She might fly into the wilderness ...'
(c) '... he cast after the Woman water like a river that She might be swept away in the flood ...'
(d) 'But the earth came to the aid of the Woman ...'
(e) 'And the dragon was wroth with the Woman ...'

Our Blessed Lady is beyond the reach of Satan, *but devotion to Her is not*, which means that (a) above represents a twofold attack by Satan: one on the devotion to Our Blessed Lady, the other on the Catholic Church itself. And now that these two are so intimately intertwined we can learn from one what happens to the other.

In order to gain some understanding of what could be meant by 'the Church in the wilderness' in (b) above, we may have a look and see what happened to devotion to Our Blessed Lady. The constant complaint of devout Catholics in relation to, say, 'Devotion to Our lady of Fatima' is, 'that you never hear about it from the pulpit ...' Our Lady of Fatima has been effectively 'sent to Coventry', i.e. sent into the wilderness, *into oblivion*. She is studiously ignored by bishops, priests, nuns and catechists, and by a great majority of the faithful. Sermons on the Rosary, on the wearing of the Scapular, have suffered a similar fate: these practices have become 'things of the past', things of 'pre-Vatican II'. In fact, the whole flourishing catholic devotion to Our Blessed Lady, which included prayer, penance, little sacrifices on Saturdays, Benedictions, processions, May and October devotions, special Masses in honour of Our Lady, it all seems to have disappeared. In so-called 'catholic' papers, on the few occasions that mention is made of Her, She is always referred to as 'Mary'. And devotion to Her is then always hedged in with 'safeguards' and 'provisos', to show the phobia, the erratic fear, of the modernistic editors and writers: 'that She might detract from Christ ...'

Their real fear of course is: that She might be effective in overcoming and taking away their idol Modernism ... so, we are not imagining that devotion to Our Blessed Lady has been sent to the wilderness: it is in the Modernists' own interest that Her sacred memory is eradicated, and trampled underfoot by the hoofs of the 200 million horses.

But since She is inalienably and inextricably bound up with the Catholic Church, it is ultimately the Catholic Church which these horsemen want to trample underfoot, and destroy, and eradicate from the face of the earth. And just as fervent devotion to Our Blessed Lady is kept alive in the overall forgetfulness by a minority of Catholic faithfuls, *so also are Catholic Faith in, and fervent love for, the Catholic Church!* The Catholic Church and the Catholic Faith in Her are positively buried under an avalanche of 'christian faith' and 'christian church', or simply 'church', propaganda. The word 'Catholic Church' has become a dirty word, a divisive word, an unhelpful and un-ecumenical term, one to be avoided at all cost, except to single Her out for ridicule ... Thousands of priests are anxious to suppress the term in their 'sermons', *except to show that the Catholic Church has gone wrong, or has accepted their modernistic heresies* ... The true Catholic Church and Her true Catholic Faith have been effectively sent into oblivion, together with Her infallible teaching, and the devotion to Our Lady. And the miracle of it all is not so much that St. John has foreseen all this nearly two thousand years ago, but has accurately seen *both* eclipses *under the one image: the Woman! The Woman in the wilderness ...*

St. John gave us undeniable proof of this. When he wrote: "... he pursued the Woman who had brought forth the male child", he left off all references to 'crying in labour pains', and so the sentence refers to both Our Lady and the Church, since both have brought forth a Male Child. One gave birth to THE male Child of all times: Christ Our Saviour, the other to THE male child of the present situation, a strong Pope, who is the Vicar of THE male Child of all times.

As for the 'river' the devil 'vomits up' after the Woman, (c) above: In the case of '*devotion to Our Lady of Fatima*', we can point to a variety of determined attempts at misleading good people into following all sorts of false, unapproved 'apparitions' which have the sole purpose of discrediting Fatima: 'sweeping it away'. This way satan makes disobedient catholics, who follow and promote all these endless and forbidden outpourings, 'fish in his own vomit to see if there is something from God in it ...'

And in the case of 'the Catholic Church', we can point to equally determined and diabolical attempts at linking the 'flood of heresies' from marxism, modernism, teilhardism, evolution, humanism with the teachings of Our Holy Mother the Catholic Church, in order to discredit the true teachings of the Catholic Church, and to 'sweep Her away in the heretical flood of satan's vomit ...'

'But the earth came to the rescue ...' (d). 'The earth' is the secular society, 'the world'. Its sins in living according to 'satan's vomit' are so obvious, that no true child of Mary and the Catholic Church can be seriously misled in believing that 'this vomit' can really be teaching emanating from the Catholic Church, not even after Vatican II ... In that way, 'the earth' came to the rescue in claiming satan's vomit as its own: 'swallowing it up ...'

Finally, 'the eagles' wings'. According to the Old Testament references attached, it must mean '*miraculous ways*' by which God will look after the ones chosen by Him to carry the Church through the terrible ordeal. Many will be martyred, but obviously many will be selected to hand over the Church intact to the next generation. They will be 'with the Church in the wilderness': *in oblivion*, looked after by God.

And so there is nothing left for satan to do but to do what God has made known to us from the very first pages of His Book: 'make war on the rest of Her seed', (e). Unable to get to the Church as a whole, satan can only from now on attack individual Catholics through persecutions. To do that, 'he stands at the sand of the sea'. 'Sea', as we have already seen previously, is 'restless humanity'. Humanity in turmoil, in the iron grip of strife, revolutions and dislocations. We only have to open our daily papers to see we have plenty of those! And out of the chaos he is calling forth his most frightful 'seed': 'the beast' ....

Twenty five centuries ago Daniel was sick for days after having seen it in action! And Christ Himself called it 'the agony of humanity'. Humanity in death throes! If its days had not been shortened, no one would have survived ...

Old Testament References in Chapter 12

Gn 37:9. [p.59]. (v.1)

He had another dream which he told his brothers. 'Look, I have had another dream', he said. 'I thought I saw the sun, the moon and eleven stars bowing to me'.

Sg 6:10. [p.1000]. (v.1)

'Who is she arising like the dawn,
fair as the moon,
resplendent as the sun,
terrible as an army set in battle array?'

Gn 3:16. [p.18]. (v.2)

To the woman He said:

'I will multiply your pains in childbearing,
You shall give birth to your children in pain'.

Mi 4:9-10. [p.1502]. (v.2)

Why are you crying aloud?
Is there no king within you?
Are your counsellors lost
that pains should grip you like a woman in labour?
Writhe, cry out, daughter of Zion,
like a woman in labour,
for now you have to leave the city
and live in the open country.
To Babylon you must go
and there you will be rescued;
there Yahweh will ransom you
out of the power of your enemies.

Dn 7:7. [p.1437]. (v.3)

Next I saw another vision in the visions of the night: I saw a fourth beast, fearful, terrifying, very strong; it had great iron teeth, and it ate, crushed and trampled underfoot what remained. It was different from the previous beasts *and had ten horns.*

Dn 8:10. [p.1439]. (v.4)

[From one of these, the small one, sprang a horn which grew to great size, towards south and east and towards the land of Splendour.] It grew right up to the armies of heaven and flung armies and stars to the ground and trampled them underfoot. It even challenged the power of the army's Prince: it abolished the Perpetual Sacrifice and overthrew the foundations of his sanctuary and the army too. It put iniquity on the sacrifice and flung truth to the ground. The horn was active and successful.

Is 66:7. [p.1246]. (v.5)

Long before being in labour
she has given birth.
Before being overtaken by birth pangs
she has been delivered of a boy.

Ps 2:9. [p.787]. (v.5)

With iron sceptre you will break them,
shatter them like potter's ware. [i.e. the nations].

Dn 10:13+. [p.1443]. (v.7)

'The prince of the kingdom of Persia has been resisting me for twenty one days, but Michael, one of the leading princes, came to my assistance. I have left him confronting the kings of Persia ...'

Dn 12:1. [p.1446]. (v.7)

'At that time Michael will stand up, the great Prince who mounts guard over your people ...'

Gn 3:1-4. [p.17]. (v.9)

The serpent was the most subtle of all the wild beasts that Yahweh God had made ... [The Story of the Fall through Deception and Disobedience, which has affected the whole world, except one.]

Gn 3:15. [p.18]. (v.13)

'I will make you enemies of each other,
you and the Woman,
your offspring and Hers.
She will crush your head,

and you will strike at Her heel.'

Ex 19:4. [p.100]. (v.14)

'You yourselves have seen what I did to the Egyptians, how I carried you on eagle's wings and brought you to Myself ...'

Is 40:31. [p.1205]. (v.14)

But those who hope in Yahweh renew their strength,
they put on wings like eagles.
They run and do not grow weary,
walk and never tyre.

Dn 7:25. [p.1438]. (v.14-17)

'... and he is going to speak words against the Most High,
and harass the saints of the Most High.
He will consider changing seasons and the Law,
and the saints will be put into his power
for a time, two times, and half a time.
But a court will be held and his power will be stripped from him, consumed, and utterly destroyed ...'

Gn 3:15. [p.18]. (v.17)

See above. The stress is here on the everlasting enmity between the Devil's seed, and the seed of the Woman.

Mt 12:50. [p.35]. (v.17)

'Anyone who does the Will of My Father in heaven, he is My brother and sister and mother.'

Chapter Seven

The Marian Dimension During the Reign of 'the Beast' Chapters Thirteen, Fourteen and Fifteen of the Apocalypse

Our world has a premonition of the advance of great evil bringing in its wake global misery. We live in the shadow of a threatening nuclear war. Rising prices, inflation, unemployment and the erosion of authority are a growing menace, and add to our toll of daily worry. The 'four evil spirits' have done a thorough job of producing universal unhappiness. Social graces, politeness, courtesy, have given way to rudeness, arrogance, impudence, loutish demands, boorish behaviour and public apathy and indifference. How strongly we are reminded here of St. Paul's words in his letter to Titus: "Remind them ... to be courteous and always polite to all kinds of people. Remember, there was a time when we too were ignorant, disobedient and misled and enslaved by different passions and luxuries; we lived then in wickedness and ill-will, hating each other and hating ourselves. *But when the kindness and love of God our Saviour were revealed for mankind, ... it was by His own compassion that He saved us.*" According to these words, the world of our days resembles the unredeemed pagan world of St. Paul, and it was, and is, no pleasure to live in it, not until the 'kindness and love of God are once again revealed to it'.

Evolution has changed our earth into a jungle, in which 'might is right', where it is the law of 'survival of the fittest', and where the unborn are mercilessly slaughtered.

Humanism has thoroughly uprooted what was still left decent by Evolution. Its one law of 'total licence' has invaded education and its quarter share of the 200 million horsemen have trampled underfoot all the children on this earth, leaving them sexually, spiritually, and socially maimed, numbed and bleeding.

Communism, when it came to China, forced the little children to pimp on their parents, and this 'evil spirit' delighted in seeing these little ones in agony, when they were coerced to kill the ones they loved, after first having betrayed them. No wonder untold thousands of them became mentally ill and deranged for life.

Modernism has done as thorough a job in the City of God as the other three did in the secular world. It has aborted 'Catholic Faith' from millions, leaving them spiritually dead. Millions of other Catholics have been spiritually paralysed after having been fed on its lethal poison without the immunity of a strong Eucharistic Life, or the antidote of a great love for the Mother of God, and without the sure-fire protection of Her Scapular and the daily Rosary! And once the breach was made, the other 'three evil spirits' invaded the City of God, and teilhardian evolution, marxism and humanism swamped catholic schools. Seminaries, sanctuaries and lecture halls, bringing to the 'Supernatural Zombies' the same 'benefits' which they had brought to the rest of the world.

And yet, all this is but the *preparation* for the reign of the beast! No wonder, then, the prophet Daniel was sick for days after he had seen it in action ... from Satan's point of view, the world is ready for its appearance. His minions have seen to that. But viewed from the Supernatural angle, the world could not be in a more helpless and pitiful state in the face of such ferocity ... Satan once again at the peak of his created might, with his evil genius at its best, fielding his strongest seed yet in a world blinded and weakened by its own pride and sins, and in which the Church has been chased into the wilderness, with war declared on the rest of Her seed ....???

And that is where Our Lady steps in ... from God's point of view too, the Church is ready for the beast's appearance ...

Section 13

The Two 'Beasts' of the Apocalypse
Chapter Thirteen of the Apocalypse

This chapter of the Apocalypse describes the appearance and activities of *two* beasts. Neither of them have actually appeared yet, so we leave the future to God. There are erudite commentaries which we can read, and which will give us some idea of what to expect.

By God's ordinance, however, we live in the times of the *preparation* for these future happenings, and that requires, as we have seen, two things:

1. *Understanding* of our times and our role in them which, together with the graces God has lavished on us will make us
2. *Effective* Instruments in His Hands for the good of the Church in our days, on which the good of the Church of the future depends.

It is mainly for an Understanding of our own times, so that we will have maximum Efficiency now, that we are encouraged by St. John to have a look at Chapter Thirteen. A description of what is happening there has a bearing on the preparations that are carried out now, and it is precisely for a good understanding of these preparations, that St. John himself invites us to take an active interest in these things. By Divine Revelation, he tells us that the beast *is a man*, a man 'with a number'. He tells us the number, and then gives everybody permission to study these matters so thoroughly, that we might come to an Understanding of the 'number'. In other words, both God and St. John want us to be 'effective' now as well as later on, and not to stumble in the dark, being a burden to every body else later on, because of our ignorance *now*. These things work both ways: if the evil being done *then* is being prepared *now*, then the good that has to be done *then*, must also be prepared *now!* Since this requires some understanding of what is GOING to happen, it certainly requires understanding of what IS happening and what SHOULD be done.

As already remarked, Chapter 13 describes the activities of TWO distinct beasts. That means there are now two types of preparation going on: one for the economic and political tyranny under the first beast; and another preparation for the religious tyranny of the second beast. Since the second beast does everything in its power to bring the world under the influence of the first beast, it looks as if the second beast needs our attention first.

St. John makes known to us 'that the second beast looks like the Lamb but speaks like the Dragon'. In appearance it masquerades as a 'christian' or maybe even 'catholic' agglomerate, but when you listen carefully to its 'gospel', it proclaims the frightful heresies of Satan.

This must make us very wary of the 'false ecumenism' of our own days. For if such a beast, such a 'church', is round the corner, then it must be in preparation now, and this rampant false ecumenism of our days would be just the thing to produce the future effect described so accurately here by St. John. It gives us a major clue as to the use that is going to be made of the Modernism of our days: make it appear that the 'modernistic church' (which, remember, tries to keep the True Bride of the Lamb of God completely buried and out of sight) is the 'catholic church', which then, for 'ecumenical reasons' will make common cause with the World Council of Churches, to make the one, united, ecumenical, christian, 'church' of the future: the 'gift' of the Holy Spirit and of Vatican II ...

This 'church' has been foreseen and foretold by a Pope and Saint of our own century, Pope St. Pius X. He has seen it so well, that he was able to give us four of its major marks and characteristics.

In *Our Apostolic Mandate*, a letter to the French Bishops of 1910 about the dangerous aberrations of a movement of initially well-meaning social catholics, the Holy Father had this to say:

> "And now overwhelmed with the deepest sadness, We ask ourselves: 'What has become of the catholicism of the Sillon?' Alas! This organisation which formerly afforded such promising expectations, has been harnessed in its course by the *modern enemies* of the Church, and now is no

> more than a miserable effluent of the great movement of apostasy, being organised in every country for the establishment of a *One-World 'Church'*, which shall have (1) neither dogma nor (2) hierarchy, neither (3) discipline of the mind nor (4) curb on the passions, and which, *under the pretext* of freedom and human dignity, would bring back to the world the reign of legalised cunning, and brute force, and the oppression of the weak, and of all those who toil and suffer.
>
> We know only too well the *dark workshops* in which are elaborated these mischievous doctrines which ought not to seduce clear-thinking minds. The leaders of the Sillon have not been able to guard against these doctrines. They have been carried away to *another gospel*, which they thought was the true Gospel of Our Saviour ..."

The 'Sillon' is dead and does not concern us here. But what about all the other startling revelations made here? A 'church'? A one-world 'church'? As the result of a universal apostasy? Which 'church' will have no dogmas, no hierarchy, no discipline of the mind and no curb on the passions? Conceived, born and shaped in the dark workshops of 'Modernism' (the 'modern' enemies of the Church), preaching 'another gospel' which will nevertheless be deceitfully passed on and received as the true Gospel of Jesus Christ? I think it is high time we catch up with this Pope, who died sixty seven year ago, but appears to be way ahead of his time ...

Even if we still feel a bit uneasy about dealing with these matters in the Apocalypse, we surely cannot quarrel with the writings of a

Pope! If this needed the bishops' immediate attention in 1910, what sort of attention does it deserve now? The Saint describes here a 'church' which will bring back to the world what we always thought were the aims and methods of *Communism*: one of the 'four evil spirits'. A 'church' in cahoots with present-day Communism? A 'church' of darkness, elaborated in the *dark* workshops of Modernism, another one of those 'four evil spirits' ... If that was the 'church' he saw take shape in his days, how far advanced do we think it is now? If the Future is capable of making us sharp-eyed for the present, how much more can the Past! And here we have BOTH the Past and the Future *converging* to make us alert for the Present.

It is obvious that this saintly Pope is defining for us the outline and the details of the second beast of St. John, and that not only with saintly Wisdom, but with Papal authority as well. He can command attention. He does demand some action. We cannot blame the Church if we are still groping in the dark.

Let us gather together the bits and pieces of information we have so far accumulated. We have 'the one-World church of darkness' of Pope St. Pius X; we have the blurred contours of an 'ecumenical agglomerate' of our times; and we have 'a second beast that looks like the Lamb but speaks like the Dragon' of St. John. Are all these the various aspects of the same 'church'?

- The 'church' of St. Pius X is certainly not the Catholic Church.
- The 'ecumenical agglomerate' of our days claims to have, Our Lord, the Holy Spirit and Vatican II on its side.

- 'The second beast of St. John' claims to look like the Lamb ...

St. Pius X accuses his 'church' of using *pretexts.* St. John reveals that his 'church' will use *pretense and deceit.* So they converge. What about the third one? Is our 'church' a transition from one into the other, or is it a genuine phase in the new 'Catholic Church'? In other words, if we help it along, are we preparing the world for Antichrist, or for the consolation of Christendom?

Genius of God! In providing us so clearly with the answer ...

I must take the reader back to Section XII on Chapter 12 of the Apocalypse where I wrote:

> "The 'Marian Dimension' has been discretely foretold to exist, openly taught to exist, and now finally shown to exist. From now on we can safely trust the Church that possess this hallmark of Perfection, this stamp of Divine favour, *and mistrust any 'church' that is without it*! That this is a stipulation of the truly Infinite Wisdom of God which has the most far-reaching consequences, we will find out in the next chapter ..."

Well, here is that place "in the next chapter" of the Apocalypse I was referring to. It is not the *claim* to the possession of the Holy Spirit, or of Christ, or of the Lamb, which distinguishes one 'church' from the next, or the True Church founded by Jesus Christ from any other 'church'. There is only one decisive feature, one foolproof characteristic: *the claim to the dearly loved 'posses-*

sion' of Our Blessed Lady. Only the Church, that has the Name of Christ's Mother engraved in the pillars of the Sanctuary of God will be recognized by God as being the Church founded by His Son ... Only the Church that made Her welcome from the start ...

We know which Church is unique in that respect.

The big question is now: 'Does the 'ecumenical agglomerate', shaping up all round us, and vying with the Catholic Church over 'recognition', have this distinctive characteristic? Does it claim love and devotion for Our Blessed Lady as its own? Does it welcome Our Lady as the Catholic Church did and still does?' The answer to this question 'has the most far reaching consequences!'

With all due respect to the Primate of all England, Cardinal Basil Hume, OSB, but I must refer my readers to an address he gave to a combined meeting of representatives of the World Council of Churches with members of the European Episcopal Conferences, [i.e. bishops, priests and 'theologians'], held in Chantilly, France, April 11-13, 1978.

During his address, Card. Hume made some extraordinary proposals:

(i) He proposed a distinction between 'Primary and Secondary Dogmas', inviting each 'church' to draw up their own lists of what THEY considered 'primary' and 'secondary', so that all this could be pooled, and a democratic vote could be taken in the near future over what could be collectively dumped as 'only secondary' by all ... *As an example of 'secondary dogmas on the Catholic side', the cardinal foreshadowed the dogmas of Our Lady!* One doesn't need much imagination to predict how the other 'churches' will react to such a generous 'catholic' lead, and which of the other 'churches' will claim retention of these dogmas out of love for Our Lady ...

(ii) He proposed that organic unity and full intercommunion should precede full unity in doctrine. Organic unity of the human body is the fullness of unity: *there is no greater unity than organic unity ...!* This, then, makes 'unity in doctrine', which the cardinal knows is impossible to obtain, completely superfluous, if full, organic unity can be obtained without it. Foremost amongst the Catholic Doctrines that would miss out completely from 'unity in doctrine' AFTER 'full, organic unity, had been obtained, would be the Dogmas on Our Blessed Lady, especially after the Primate of all England declared them publicly to be 'of only secondary importance' ...

With this speech, Cardinal Hume, in one stroke, barred forever the 'ecumenical church' he is building from laying claims to equality with the True Church because of the absence of Our Lady from the 'church' he and his European friends envisage. Of that 'church' Our Blessed Lady could neither be the Mother nor the Model or Type. In the cardinal's mind (as in the mind of his predecessor Cranmer), the Catholic Church as we know it can be dispensed with, to make room for some hybrid 'one-world church', foreseen by Pope St. Pius X. That makes this 'church'-without-dogma, which the cardinal here proposes, the 'missing link' between the 'church-without-dogma' described by Pope St. Pius X and the 'church of the second beast': the 'church of the WCC'.

We can now better appreciate that a knowledge of the predictions of St. John, (future), and a knowledge of the teachings of the Church, (past), have a bearing on our lives *now*, 'with far-reaching consequences'.

Obviously, there is much more to it than this. A speech like the cardinal's does not come 'out of the blue'. A lot of 'testing of feelings' has gone on in a wide cross section in and out of the Church, before it is delivered with so much confidence of success. Coinciding with this speech by Cardinal Hume was a similar one by a Jesuit in America, delivered to a big 'ecumenical' seminar there ...

But, what the cardinal and this Jesuit should have known, or if they knew, they did not take us into their confidence about it, is, that the World Council of Churches in its 1961 New Delhi meeting had already decided, that this envisaged 'universal church' *is not to be built around the Son of Mary*, but around the 'cosmic christ' of Teilhard de Chardin! This means that in the proposed 'unity' not only will Our Blessed Lady be absent, but also the Second Person of the Blessed Trinity, Our Lord and Saviour, Jesus Christ. In the absence of the Mother, *the Son in not present either!* And the 'church' is going to be built around the feverish illusions of an evolutionary imagination ...

This proves conclusively that once again *'The Marian Dimension'* is the deciding factor in the thirteenth Chapter of the Apocalypse. No matter how much the diabolical 'church' of the second beast may *look* like the Lamb: no matter how many cardinals, bishops, priests, nuns, layfolk support it then, and are working for it

NOW, the glaring absence of Our Blessed Lady is the surest sign of the equally glaring absence of our beloved Saviour, Jesus Christ. As already said before: this has far-reaching consequences. What we do NOW, in the time of preparation, will be of momentous importance by the time humanity, and the Church, have reached 'the thirteenth Chapter of the Apocalypse', and are confronted by the second beast 'which looks like the Lamb but speaks like the dragon'. If it speaks 'like the dragon' then, it is doing it now! If only we care to listen carefully ....

It should no longer come as a surprise to us, then, that it is not 'the beast' which will dominate the time of his appearance, but Our Blessed Lady! Her children will not be impressed by the false signs and wonders performed by him, or in his name. They will resist all attempts to make them worship the beast or his image, they will not be misled by the permeation of lying and false teaching, and they will refuse to accept 'his number' anywhere on their bodies. This needs much preparation and careful planning now, much prayer and study. Many in those days will depend on 'the seed of the Woman' to give a lead and to show understanding and courage and great confidence in God. For it will be given only to those to finally lead all the others to victory.

This is all we really need to know now. This will give us plenty to do to consolidate our own consecration to Our Lady, and to help others to discover it for themselves, in whatever time is left, the immense benefits hidden in the subjection to Her sweet dominion, especially during the 'reign of the beast'.

From here on we can only have a bird's eye view of the rest of this remarkable book, still largely covered with the mist of the future, but with the Marian peaks rising high above it, aglow with the glory of God's Sun.

Before we leave this chapter, I think it will be to the consolation of the reader to be shown that, to my way of thinking, there is still another strong reference to Our Blessed Lady built into the final verse by that wonderful seer, St. John! By God's grace, *nothing* escaped his far-seeing, penetrating gaze ... In that verse, St. John reveals 'the number of the beast', and invites everybody to show intelligence and ponder about it.

Everybody???

The final verse mentions the number of the beast as being 'six hundred and sixty six', what is being said is, 'that this person knows you intimately'. He knows your strength and your weaknesses. 'You cannot put it over him!'

In the 'number of the beast' there is at least one 'six'. No matter what the other digits stand for, the last digit stands for 'six'. Nobody, as yet, knows the meaning of this 'number', but it appears that 'an important six' is connected with it.

Therefore, if I were asked: 'What, in your opinion, is the most important 'six' of this century?' I would have no hesitation in answering: 'The SIX Apparitions of Our Lady at Fatima ...' Fatima again ... So, it is not a 'he' who holds 'the number of the beast': it is a 'She'. It is 'the Woman of Genesis'. Fatima is so central in the whole resistance to 'the beast', that it did not escape St. John. Our Lady of Fatima is part of that magnificent vision with which the previous chapter began: 'A great sign appeared in Heaven ...'

And just as Our Blessed Lady and Her Replica, the Catholic Church, did not want 'everybody' to know 'the Third Secret of Fatima', so also will Our Blessed Lady not reveal the 'secrets' of the number of the beast to everybody, but only takes into Her confidence: 'to know the beast intimately', those who, in their struggle with him, have strengthened the Church by their great devotion to Her. St. John is quite adamant about this: 'There is need for WISDOM here ...', he says. Now Wisdom is the First Gift of the Holy Spirit and is learnt at the 'Seat of Wisdom': Our Blessed Lady, the Spouse of the Holy Spirit.

"The beast cannot put it over 'The Woman'", and She will see to it, that he cannot put it over *'Her seed'*.

Our Lady of Fatima appeared on the 13th of each month, from May till October, in 1917. Some people have brought to our attention that this number 13 reminds us of the *13th Station* in the Stations of the Cross, where Our Blessed Lady receives the lifeless Body of the Lamb of God on Her lap, after He had paid the price for our sins. It was here, in the agony of this tearful moment, that She too paid a price, the price of Her 'Second Fiat': to become the Mother of the Church, the Mystical Body of the Son on Her lap.

Maybe we can extend the vision here, and be reminded, that with this same number 13, Our Blessed Lady also draws our attention to *the 13th Chapter of the Book of Revelation*, where Her Daughter, Our Holy Mother the Catholic Church, will receive the lifeless bodies of many Martyrs under Antichrist on Her lap, after they too had paid the high price for the frightful sins of the same ungrateful world. Mary, Mother *and Model* of the Church ...

Old Testament References in Chapter 13

At several verses of this Chapter quotes from the Seventh Chapter of Daniel will be made. The reader is advised to read the whole of that chapter first, and keep it handy for further consultation.

Is 57:20. [p. 1234]. (v.1)

The wicked however are like the restless sea
that cannot be still,
and washes up mud and slime.
'No peace', says my God, 'for the wicked'.

Dn 7:2. [p.1436]. (v.1)

'I saw that the four winds of heaven were stirring up the great sea; four great beasts emerged from the sea, each different from the other ...'

Dn 2:3-7. [p.1436]. (v.2)

'The first was like a LION ... The second beast I saw was like a BEAR ... After this I looked and saw another beast like a LEOPARD ... Next I saw a fourth beast, fearful, terrifying, very strong ... It had ten horns ...'

Jr 27:6-8. [p.1296]. (v.3,4)

'For the present, I have handed all these countries over to Nebuchadnezzar, king of Babylon, My servant; I have even put the wild animals at his service. All the nations will be subject to him, to his son and to his grandson, until the time for his own country comes in its turn, when mighty nations and great kings will enslave him. Any nation or kingdom that will not submit to Nebuchadnezzar, king of Babylon, and will not bow its neck to

the yoke of the king of Babylon, I shall punish with sword, famine and plague – it is Yahweh who speaks – until I have delivered it into his power ...
11. The nation however that bends its neck to the yoke of the king of Babylon and submits to him, I shall leave in peace on its own soil – it is Yahweh who speaks – to farm it and stay in it.'

Dn 11:36+ [p.1445-6]. (v.5-8)

[Here is one early fulfilment of the prophecies given to, and made by, Daniel, as a prefiguration of what is still to come. In several places, Daniel clearly indicates these prophecies are related *'to the time of the End'*. And the rise and fall of Antiochus clearly did not occur 'at the time of the End'. The beast of the Apocalypse, with the markings of Daniel clearly attached to it, shows conclusively that Daniel saw immediate and distant future under *one* image, as is so often the case.]

Jr 15:2. [p.1277]. (v.10)

And if they ask you, 'Where shall we go?', tell them this.
"Yahweh says this:
Those for the plague, to the plague;
Those for the sword, to the sword;
Those for famine, to famine;
Those for captivity, into captivity.
Four kinds of doom I consign to them ..."

Dt 13:2-4. [p.236]. (v.13-15)

'If a prophet or a dreamer of dreams arises among you and offers to do a sign or wonder for you, and the sign or wonder comes about; and if he then says to you, "Come then, let us follow other gods, (whom you have not known) and serve them", you are not to listen to the words of the prophet or to the dreams of that dreamer. *Yahweh your God is testing you* to know if you love Yahweh your God with all your heart and all your soul. Yahweh your God you shall follow, Him you shall fear, His commandments you shall keep, His voice you shall obey, Him you shall serve, to Him you shall cling ...'

Dn 3:5-7 [p.1426]. (v.14-15) and

Dn 3:15f,

The story of the three young men in the fiery furnace because they refused to bow the knee for the statue, putting all their trust in God. Compelling reading at this part of the Apocalypse, both for an idea of the forthcoming cruelty as for an example of God's saving power during the reign of the beast.

Section 14

'Virgins Unaffected by the Beast'
Harvest of His Followers
Chapter Fourteen of the Apocalypse

One of the hardest things to maintain is the virtue of Hope in times of great distress and depravity. Providentially for us, the Supernatural, Infused, Divine Virtue of Hope, by which we share in God's Nature, and which is given to us in Baptism, is altogether out of reach of human nature, can neither be obtained nor maintained by natural means, and depends on prayer and the frequent use of the Sacraments for its growth and maturity. Since it is the *second* of the three Divine Virtues, it depends on Catholic Faith for its existence and strength, since Catholic Faith is the Supernatural Light, in which 'the things hoped for can be seen.' (Hebr. 11:1). The stronger the Light of Faith the better we can 'see' the Supernatural Realities which reassure us, and give strength and meaning to our Hope.

Catholics who, in times of material affluence, have learned to depend on their bank account instead of on God, will find out in times of uncertainty and scarcity, that it is not 'big enough' to see them through, and they get worried and touchy because falling back on God is unfamiliar to them. "Blessed are the poor ...". They always had to turn to God and so it became a *habit*: the *virtue* of Hope.

The erosion of Catholic Faith can be measured from the loss of the Divine Virtue of Hope in our modern world. If 70% of Catholic women are 'on the Pill', then 70% of Catholic fathers and mothers no longer had their hope and trust vested in God, thereby exposing their lack of Catholic Faith in the Catholic Church's teachings.

When God wrote *Humanae Vitae* (let there be no misunderstanding: it was God Who gave this saving document to the Church, and through Her to the whole world), He had before Him all the slums on earth, and all the poor, the strugglers, the battlers and the outcasts that live in them. He knew each one by name, and He knew the circumstances of each. And out of the depth of the Infinite Goodness of His Divine Nature, He poured forth the saving, liberating Grace of *Humanae Vitae.* For He knew, *if that saving Truth was accepted with only a grain of True Faith*, He Himself would enter into those lives as only a God can, and sweep aside the innumerable obstacles and mountains of difficulties that lack of Faith and fear had created.

Because they were poor He gave them Humanae Vitae. No poor should go through their poverty alone ...

And before the same Divine Eyes were also the rich and the well-to-do of the West, who had His saving teaching for more than 1900 years. To them, the same liberating, redeeming Grace of *Humanae Vitae* was also offered, in order that its acceptance in Faith would *really* set free the Third World hungry *because of the ubiquity of the Mystical Body.*

But the West demurred, poisoned by a freely accepted 'philosophy of corruption'. The Faith of bishops, priests, 'theologians', of the well-to-do and the affluent, of nuns, brothers and of 'educated' lay people was lacking, *and the Graces attached to this Saving Truth remained unclaimed and unearned!* And the Third World missed out ... And no amount of marxism, liberation 'theology', massive projects of contraceptives and abortions is going to make up for it.

The immense force of the Omnipotent, invading the lives of mere mortals to take over its direction, and to lift them over mountains of difficulties on the quivering, but sustained: "*I believe, Lord, help my unbelief!*", is DENIED to women who are encouraged to stay on the pill by the timidity and silence of the clergy, born out of a 'belief': 'that it is better not to rock the boat'. On what 'philosophy', on what 'reasoning' is the miserable opposite to the Immensity of God's all-powerful Grace considered BETTER, more true, than God's Word itself that was spoken to us through *Humanae Vitae*? On the same 'philosophy' which made thousands of religious, priests and 'theologians' flock out of the Church in embrace of the world in the mistaken belief that Vatican II had given them the green light for that. The same 'philosophy' which is driving the whole world inexorably to its final confrontation with the ultimate in evil ... The same 'philosophy' as the one of the 'church of darkness': the 'philosophy' of Teilhard de Chardin. A 'philosophy' of *evolution*: one of the 'four evil spirits'.

If 'the Pill' is a 'mark of the beast', then Teilhard de Chardin is a 'prophet of Antichrist'.

But God would not be God, if 'the church of darkness', if 'the false ecumenism' and 'the great movement of apostasy' were the end of the story. If He had not given to His friends and to His Church *the ultimate weapon.*

And so we finally made our way in the presence of Her whom sinner and Saint, in agony and ecstasy, has graced with the everlasting name: Our Holy Mother the Catholic Church. *Like Our Lady*, the Church grew in years, but never wrinkled. She is still the youthful, spotless Bride of the Lamb of God, the Holy One, the Faithful One. Over the centuries She has done what Her Divine Founder and Groom had wanted Her to do: to bear Him children, many children; to fill 'His Father's House' from the ends of the earth.

She instructed them in purity of doctrine, in poverty of spirit, in obedience to the Father's word. And the Son of God loved Her. He adorned Her with His most precious jewels, He entrusted to Her care His most priceless possessions: His Body, His Blood, His Grace, His Heart, His Truth, His infinite Mercy, the Mysteries of His Divine Knowledge, the Honour of His Holy Mother. He cared for Her as never a groom cared for a bride.

And in return the Church loved the Lamb of God with an eternity of love. For Him She loved the sinner as much as the Saint. She taught the ignorant as well as the learned. She strengthened the Martyr to stand form till the end. She consoled the bereaved, prepared the dying, and cared for the poor and the sick, the orphan and the widow, the heathen and the lost. She was all to all. She will never be under the control of iniquity nor under the command of men. She can live under any system, outlast any enemy, survive any evil. For the Church does not rest on human counsels nor on the councils of the world. Her Head is divine, so is Her Life. She has no need to speak with the voice of this world to be heard.

For within Her is the pearl of great beauty for which the merchant-in-the-know sacrificed everything in order to possess it: CATHOLIC FAITH, the most precious gift of Almighty God to finite little man. For it is through that Faith, and that Faith alone, that we know Him, His Son and His Holy Spirit; His Mother, His Church and the Bodily presence of His Son in the Blessed Eucharist; and also his Face in the poor, and His Truth in *Humanae Vitae.*

Catholic Faith will never die out on earth. It will never disappear from this earth. It will never cease to have consequences on this earth: fruits of Redemption and eternal Salvation. Fruits of prayer and penance, of great Hope and great Love. Fruits of conversion to Her from whom this Faith was received in the first place: *Our Holy Mother the Catholic Church.*

But in the caring for the children of the Lamb of God, there grew in Her own heart but one desire, a desire so secret that it never left the place where it was born for fear that it would be revealed. But against Her will the desire grew, and finally the Bridegroom read it in Her eyes, the unspoken secret between them in the intimate union of their Mystical Life. She loved the Lamb of God; Se had studied Him in His Life on earth; She understood His every mood. She had seen His Birth, and imitated His poverty. She had seen His Hidden Life, and imitated His Obedience and Love for His Parents. She had followed Him in His travels whilst preaching the Kingdom of God, and Her own missionaries had gone out to the four corners of the earth. The union of love between the Bridegroom and His Bride had grown strong and in the chaste intimacy between the Son of God and His Catholic Church, the secret could no longer be kept. Had not St. Paul compared the union of the Christian marriage to the union between Christ and His Church? And the Creator of Christian Marriage understood ...

Faithfully, His Bride had taught every young bride that came before Her altar to be joined in holy wedlock 'to have her man and to hold': to hold onto him for better or for worse, to follow him wherever he may go. To suffer with him whatever would be his fate. And the Church watched them go ... And the desire in Her own heart grew stronger. Would she alone, in all Eternity, be a Bride, espoused to a Man who for love of Her let Himself be crucified, without having shared the experience with Him? Would She alone not be allowed to show Her love '*in fine*': till the very end? Would She alone be the only Bride not knowing what it is: '*exinanivit Semetipsum*', 'He emptied Himself'? She had seen Him in His agony, She had watched Him being scourged, crowned with thorns, mocked, spat upon, rejected. She had meditated on His last journey on earth, carrying His Cross all the way to Calvary out of Love for Her; seen His final, all-embracing Sacrifice, laying down His Life for His sheep, and how His Holy Mother shared every suffering with Him. And the Love in Her own heart became infinite ... If only somehow, somehow, She could do the same, share with Him, show Her love for Him and for Her children, *their* children, to the same extent: 'in fine'. For every Martyr She had sustained, his hour had finally arrived. Would *Her Hour* ever come? To hear Herself being condemned to death, and then at last be permitted to follow in the bleeding footsteps of the Man She had adored in so much love? All the way to Her own execution, He own annihilation? To give Her life for Him. She had faithfully imitated His every example. Would oh would there be given Her, before the End, *One* chance, Her chance, to pay Him back; to imitate 'in fine', till the end ...

And the Father of all understood.

And in His infinite Wisdom and Love, He found a way ...

The Jewish leaders once said amongst themselves: "We don't like this Christ and His message. We want one in our own image, a message to our liking". They did not like the Messiah as sent by God and promised by the Prophets. He had to be 'improved'. He had to be 'renewed'. As He was, He had to be done away with. And when they had finished remodelling Him 'after their own image and liking', *He had to be buried* ... On the Cross He had become their image. He finally looked like them, as they were known to the Father: disfigured and killed by Sin ... But only then the miracle had been wrought: through His frightful Passion and Death, sustained by an Infinite Love, *they themselves, not Him had been renewed, redeemed!* In the Heavenly Beauty of the Supernatural Life, they could look again as the adopted children of God, in true likeness of His Son Jesus Christ. And out of His pierced Heart, washed in His water and Blood, the new creation was born: His Church, His very own Bride.

As the last one in a long line of break-aways down history, 'Modern Man' too has raised his voice to God and said:

> "We don't like this Catholic Church as handed down to us through the ages. We want her changed. We want Her renewed after our own image. Her message changed after our own liking, along the beautiful lines of Teilhard de Chardin, who allows us to embrace the world ..."

And God saw the pitiful state to which 'evolution' has reduced 'modern man': 'an irrational animal, let loose in nature, groping his way through endless trial and error, because he doesn't know enough history, enough religion, enough prayer' (Lammerts). And remembering the dearest wish of His Son's Bride on earth, and remembering the true renewal: Redemption, that had been brought about by the Death of His Son on the Cross, He relented.

"And their cries gained the upperhand ..."

The hour of the Church had finally come. Which then reveals the most intimate purpose of the teilhardian 'church of darkness': to be the harlot church, the 'Barabbas', preferred by 'modern man' in preference to the spotless Bride of the Lamb of God, our Holy Mother the Catholic Church. And the fury of hell unleashed against the Catholic Church will then be such, that St. John could write in his Apocalypse, 'And it was given to it to make war with the Saints *and to conquer them* ...' And that Daniel could predict in the Spirit, 'that the Perpetual Sacrifice will be abolished for three and a half years', the exact time-span allotted by St. John to the reign of the Beast.

But the Catholic Church will not die out altogether. Not all the Catholic will be annihilated. But their hidden existence will eclipse the Church for a while, like the stone before the Holy Sepulchre his for a while that other Sacred Body of Our Lord ... They will be hidden in the New Ark, the Marian Dimension, carrying them safely over the Deluge of Terror unleashed on earth during the reign of the Beast. The Good Friday of the Church will be terrible, but the One Who sustained Her Son on the Day of His Crucifixion, has now been officially appointed by the Second Vatican Council to sustain the Church on Hers.

For the Bride of the Lamb of God, and out of love for that same sinful humanity that crucified Her Groom, the same hour has at last arrived. Now His Bride wishes to go through the same experience, through the same Good Friday, for the sake of 'modern man': that pathetic end-product of a faked evolution.

Is that a crime? Is that so confusing? Does that make Her weak? So that we should be ashamed of Her, go our own way, calling ourselves 'christians' and no longer Catholic? Does that give us the right to push Her aside, follow our own 'beliefs' and passions, because the Church no longer seems to know what She is doing?

The time and the hour has come, that the world will select the 'harlot': the 'teilhardian church of darkness' in preference to Her. So that the Church can suffer what Christ went through when that same humanity cast Him aside in preference for a robber and murderer. And then at last will the Catholic Church be able to show Her love for God and men 'in fine', till the end. And go the same painful way to Her own Calvary. But just like Her Groom, the Church is still beautiful and infinitely powerful. She will rise again and conquer the earth, because a Church in such love is the most powerful thing on earth: irresistible.

There are many silent, timid, confused bishops. They are wounding the Church, oh yes. The Church feels it, like Christ did. Christ suffered. So does His Church. For the vast teilhardian church of darkness, in its thirst for power over the Catholic Church, is, in its blindness, as the Second Beast actively engaged in hastening the global enslavement under Antichrist. But when this harlot-church will be handed over to 'the Beast' to make it appear as if finally Antichrist and Satan are ruling over the Catholic Church, when they dominate this vast, one-world anti-church with its anti-pope, then the *machinery* of the Catholic Church may appear to be there. But the Bride of the Lamb of God will be safely under the protection of Her, appointed by God at this hour, Her Hour, to be the Mother of the Church.

And when the Church knows what it is 'to be the Bride of the Lamb of God', then the same conquering Powers will make Her irresistible to the powers and forces of Darkness. At the moment of Her greatest desertion and seeming annihilation, She will prove to be the true Daughter of God the Father: indestructible. And if we will be proud of Her then, and flock to Her in love, we should stay with Her now, in Her moment of greatest desertion, when She needs all of us most ...

"For She is a breath of the Majesty of God,
Pure emanation of the Glory of the Almighty,

Hence nothing impure can touch Her.
She is the reflection of the Eternal light,
Untarnished mirror of God's active power,
The image of His perfection.
Although alone, She can do all.
Herself unchanging, She makes all things new.
In each generation She enters into holy souls,
Forming them into friends of God, and prophets.
For God loves only those who live with Wisdom.
She indeed is more splendid than the sun;
She outshines all the constellations
Compared with light, She takes precedence,
For light must yield to night,
But over Wisdom evil will never triumph!
She deploys Her strength from one end of the earth to the other.
It is She who orders all things for good." (Wisdom 7:25-8:1)

The ability to apply these inspired words initially to Our Blessed Lady, (in ch.2), the Model and Proto-type of the Church, and here, with equal validity, to the Catholic Church herself, as Her most perfect Daughter, shows that in the great battle to be fought, and the great victory to be obtained, Mother and Daughter are, in the Mind and the intentions of God, but one. In Paradise, God had included the children with the Woman, the Head and the members of the Mystical Body, to whom the Woman had given birth.

It is this Faith, this sure knowledge, *which is the foundation of the Hope* with which the Catholic Church enters the most crucial times of Her existence. In this Chapter Fourteen of the Apocalypse, the most dire consequences are predicted for those who accept the mark of the beast. Therefore, Catholics must have the gravest of reasons not to submit to the pressure: political, economic, social, religious, or whatever other, to accept 'the mark' in order to survive ...That means that they must be given *NOW*, in the time of the training and preparation, the same gravest of reasons *not to embrace the 'philosophy'*, whereby millions of catholic women have already succumbed to accept, even before his official appearance, 'a mark of the beast': the contraceptive pill.

To help them overcome their fears and forebodings in the face of the most ugly intimidation possible, St. John shows all of us that, at that most fearful time, there will be on earth 'Virgins' who have taken the Lamb and the Church at their word, have entrusted to God their whole being and existence, and have come through the ordeal 'with flying colours', even with their virginity intact ... In other words: it is possible. Many of us are not fighters, not like the ones mentioned in the next chapter, and those of us who are not, would like to know how to go about our business without drawing attention to ourselves, and without compromise to our principles and the wellbeing of others. The problems are very basic and down-to-earth.

'To what schools can we safely send our children?
'What outings, what camps can they go to?
'What entertainment is allowable?
'What books can they read?' ....

The list is endless, the answers are becoming very restrictive. Everywhere the freedoms they get from the Humanists are 'free rides on the road to Hell':

> Freedom of total expression,
> freedom to do what they like,
> freedom to experiment with sex and drugs,
> freedom to sue their parents for being born, for being 'forced into a religion' as a child,
> freedom to run away from home, to have abortions on demand, to have access to 'the pill', to watch, read, say what they like ...
> And finally, the greatest 'freedom' of them all: 'freedom from their parents', 'compulsory' euthanasia.

The problems are not new to the Church. She was there to help and inspire the newly made converts in the decadent Roman civilisation. What an environment to start a new Religion, a young Church ... It proved to be a great success! If that same Religion doesn't look so exciting and new and absorbing anymore, it is because there are so many watered-down versions of it around; because it hasn't really been tried out for us in adverse conditions, in a hostile environment. But the inbuilt appeal to greatness, to holiness and mastery are still there, to be unlocked and released when the pressure is on. Unlocked now, by 'the Key of David', in the pressures of today...

We are living at present in a tough training school, where 'the Woman' is inspiring us, Her children, to live on our natural and supernatural wits '*with Her, in the desert*' ... We learn what it means to be diplomatic without compromise, to trust without being naive, to be stern without being inflexible. We are constantly asked to differentiate between the most revolting sins and the most revolting sinners; to wrest precious preys from the mouths of lions and bears, creatures of the 'wilderness' in which 'modernism' forces us to live. And some 'daring' bits and pieces of Holy Scripture are beginning to stick in our minds; they refuse to leave because they are starting to make sense, here in the desert. Words, such as:

> "But for Your sons, not even the fangs of venomous serpents could bring them down;
> Your mercy came to their aid and cured them.
> One sting – how quickly healed! – to remind them of Your Commandments,
> rather than that, by sinking into deep forgetfulness,
> they should be cut off from Your kindness." (Wis. 16:10-11)

This text taken from the Book of Wisdom should be of particular consolation to the parents of today and tomorrow. It refers to an event during the 40-year sojourn of the Israelites 'in the wilderness', in search of the Promised Land after the Exodus from Egypt. The following account of this event is taken from the Book of Numbers.

> "They left Mount Hor by the road to the Sea of Suph to skirt the land of Edom. On the way the people lost patience. They spoke against God and against Moses. 'Why did you bring us out of Egypt to die in this wilderness? For there is neither bread nor water here; we are sick of this unsatisfying food'.

[Many children, teenagers and young adults from good Catholic homes have given up 'going to Mass on Sundays', encouraged by a deceitful catechetics and in the mistaken belief that there is neither bread nor water there to satisfy their spiritual hunger; and they have discontinued the practise of receiving Holy Communion: that Divine Food from Heaven.]

"At this God sent fiery serpents among the people; their bite brought death to many in Israel.

[We are reminded here of the 200 million 'serpent's tails with heads' which have been let loose amongst us! Their bite too has brought spiritual death to countless catholics...]

"The people came and said to Moses, 'We have sinned by speaking against Yahweh and against you, Intercede for us with Yahweh to save us from these serpents'.

[We too can go to Someone to intercede for us with God: Mary!]

"Moses interceded for the people and Yahweh answered him, 'Make a fiery serpent and put it on a standard. If anyone is bitten and looks at it, he shall live'.

[We too can look up and see 'THE serpent' under Mary's feet and confidently ask Her to be cured of its bite.]

Rereading again the text quoted above from the Book of Wisdom, we see that parents of today can still have great confidence in God and His Holy Mother, even if their children have been bitten by the frightful sex education unleashed by one 'snake', or by the immoral 'catechetics' unleashed by another. Their Catholic Faith, their Catholic Hope and Love, their Rosaries, Scapular and acts of penance will obtain the 'quick cure from God' promised here.

> "They will pick up snakes in their hands,
> and be unharmed should they drink deadly poison." (Mk.16:18)

> "Yes, I have given you power to tread underfoot serpents and scorpions and the whole strength of the enemy. Nothing shall ever hurt you. Yet do not rejoice that the spirits submit to you; rejoice rather that your names are written in heaven. (Lk.10:19-20)

> "You need not fear the terrors of the night,
> the arrow that flies in daytime,
> the plague that stalks in the dark,
> the scourge that wreaks havoc in broad daylight.
> "Though a thousand fall at your left,
> ten thousand at your right hand,
> you yourself will remain unscathed,
> with His faithfulness for shield and buckler.
> "No disaster can overtake you,
> no plague come near your tent:
> He will put you in His Angels' charge

> to guard you wherever you go.
> "They will support you in their hands
> in case you hurt your foot on a stone;
> *you will tread on asp and adder,*
> *trample on savage lions and dragons.*
> "'I rescue all who cling to Me, I protect whoever knows My Name. I answer everyone who invokes Me, I am with them when they are in trouble; I bring them safety and honour'." (Ps.91:5-15)

Yes, 'life if the desert', where the oases of good sermons and good Catholic books are few and far between, is tough, and much of its goodness depends on the use we make of our Supernatural Wits, reinforced by biblical quotes such as printed above. But we have one great consolation: life in the other camp must be living death itself. For we have 'the Woman' with us: Our Blessed Lady and Our Holy Mother the Catholic Church. And since She lives 'in the Sanctuary', we also have the Eucharistic Lamb with us, who directs everything according to His Father's Will.

We have Supernatural protection: the Holy Rosary. And last but not least: we have '*Supernatural Immunity*': the Holy Scapular. In this we have the antidote for the hostile environment in which we are forced to live; no, *asked to live* by an Omniscient Father, 'Who is with us when we are in trouble and brings us safety and honour'.

These, then, are the answers we get to the questions we put earlier regarding the safety of our children. There were no catholic schools in ancient Rome, no catholic hospitals, no catholic institutions. There was no catholic press, and there were no catholic libraries. So, if we have to do without any of those, remember: then, there was not even a Catholic precedent! Immorality and depravity were rife. Yet, the Church thrived. She did protect her children, looked after them and gave them all the Food and Immunity they needed at their tender age. She is doing the same again, but now we have the inestimable advantage of '*the Marian Dimension*' in case we might wonder where the True Church is.

Old Testament References in Chapter 14

2K 19:30f. [p.481]. (v.1)

"The surviving remnant of the House of Judah
shall bring forth new roots below and fruits above;
for a remnant shall go out from Jerusalem,
and survivors from Mount Zion.
The jealous love of Yahweh will accomplish this."

Jl 3:5. [p.1474]. (v.1)

All who call on the Name of Yahweh will be saved,
For on Mount Zion there will be some who escaped,
as Yahweh has said,
and in Jerusalem some survivors whom Yahweh will call.

Ob 17. [p.1492]. (v.1)

But on Mount Zion there will be some who have escaped
- it shall become a holy place -
and the House of Jacob will despoil
its own despoilers.

Zp 3:12-13. [p.1525]. (v.1,5)

In your midst I will leave

a humble and lowly people,
and those who are left in Israel
will seek refuge in the Name of Yahweh.
They will do no wrong,
will tell no lies;
and the perjured tongue will no longer
be found in their mouths.
But they will be able to graze and rest
with no one to disturb them.

Ps 33:3. [p.814]. (v.3)

Sing a new song in His honour,
play with all your skill as you acclaim Him

Ps 98:1. [p.881]. (v.3)

Sing Yahweh a new song
for He has performed marvels,
His own right hand, His holy arm,
gives Him the power to save.

Is 42:10. [p.1208]. (v.3)

Sing a new hymn to Yahweh.
Let His praise resound from the ends of the earth.
Let the sea and all that it holds sing His praises.

Is 43:19. [p.1211]. (v.3)

See, I am doing a new deed,
even now it comes to light: can you not see it?
Yes, I am making a road in the wilderness
paths in the wilds.
The wild beasts will honour Me
jackals and ostriches.

because I am putting water in the wilderness
rivers in the wilds,
to give My chosen people drink.
The people I have formed for Myself
will sing My praises.

Jr 2:2-3. [p.1250]. (v.4)

Yahweh says this:
'I remember the affection of your youth,
the love of your bridal days:
You followed Me through the wilderness,
through a land unsown.
Israel was sacred to Yahweh,
the first fruits of His harvest;
anyone who ate of it had to pay for it!
Misfortune came to them ...'

Zp 3:13. [p.1520]. (v.5)

See above.

Dn 3:4. [p.1426]. (v.6)

(Proclamation to the 'Men of all peoples, nations, languages', to prostrate themselves and worship the king's statue.)

Ex 20:11. [p.102]. (v.7)

For in six days Yahweh made the heavens and the earth,
and the sea and all that these hold.

Is 21:9. [p.1174]. (v.8)

Look, here come the cavalry,
horsemen two by two.
They spoke to me; they said,
'Fallen, fallen is Babylon,

and all the images of her gods
are shattered to the ground'.

Is 51:17f. [p.1226]. (v.8)

Awake, awake!
On your feet Jerusalem!
You who from Yahweh's hand have drunk
the cup of His wrath;
See, I take out of your hand
the chalice of My wrath;
you shall drink it no longer.
I will put it into the hand of your tormentor.

Jr 25:15. [p.1294]. (v.8ff)

Yahweh the God of Israel said this to me.
'Take this cup of wine from My hand,
and make all the nations to whom I send you, drink it.
Let them drink and reel and lose their wits
at the sword I am sending among them ...
For I will next summon a sword
against all the inhabitants of the earth'.

Gn 19:28. [p.36). (v.10f)

Rising early in the morning,
Abraham went to the place where he had stood before Yahweh,
and looking towards Sodom and Gomorrah, and across all the plain,
he saw the smoke rising from the land, like smoke from a furnace

Is 34:9f. [p.1195]. (v.10f)

Its streams turn into pitch

its dust into brimstone,
its land becomes blazing pitch.
Never quenched night or day
its smoke goes up forever,
it shall lie waste age after age,
no one will pass through it.

Jl 4:12f. [p.1475]. (v.14f)

'Let the nations rouse themselves, let them march
to the Valley of Jehosaphat,
for I am going to sit in judgement there
on all the nations round.
Put the sickle in, the harvest is ripe;
come and tread, the winepress is full,
the vats are overflowing,
so great is their wickedness!'

Dn 7:13. [p.1437]. (v.14)

I gazed into the visions of the night,
and I saw coming on the clouds of heaven,
one like a Son of man.
He came to the One of great age
and was led into His presence.
On Him was conferred sovereignty ...

Is 63:1-6. [p.1242]. (v.14ff)

'Who is this coming from Edom,
from Bozrah in garments stained with crimson,
so richly clothed, marching so full of strength?'
'It is I, who speak of integrity
and am powerful to save.'

'Why are Your garments red,
Your clothes as if You had trodden the winepress?'
'I have trodden the winepress alone.
Of the men of my people not one was with Me.
In My anger I trod them down,
trampled them in My wrath.
Their juice spattered My garments
and all My clothes are stained.
For in My heart was a day of vengeance,
My year of Redemption had come ...'
'I looked: there was no one to help;
Not one could I find to support Me.
My own arm then was My mainstay,
My wrath My support.
I crushed the people in My fury,
trampled them in My anger,
and made the juice of them run all over the ground.'

Section 15

'Those Who Fought the Beast and Won'
God's War on the Wicked
Chapter Fifteen of the Apocalypse
"*The Glory of the Church Militant*"

Just as Antiochus Epiphanes, the first fulfilment of 'the beast' that Daniel saw in action, is a forerunner of the 'beast of the Apocalypse', so also is the Jewish Resistance against this 'first beast' a model and type of the Resistance of the Church against Antichrist, spoken of here in the Apocalypse. The Two Books of the Maccabees are thus a source of great illumination for all those who, through the direction of the Eucharistic Lamb, find themselves shouldered with the task of pitting their resourcefulness and their ingenuity against the ominous might of 'the beast'. The 'Church Militant' cannot live up to that Name without a fight. Without a great Resistance Movement. An Underground. Like in the Book of Maccabees: the signal comes from God. No one starts the 'holy war' prematurely on his own. No one, after the signal has been flashed, may refuse service.

It is certainly not the intention to let the previous Section give the impression that all we have to do is 'lie low in the wilderness', count a certain number of days and all will eventually turn out alright. The Books of the Maccabees tell us a different story. The war came to 'the desert'. The previous chapter gave us Hope and Faith in God and in our Blessed Lady by showing us that it is possible *to survive.* This present chapter must show us further, that is is also possible *to win!* The previous chapter supplied us with a 'spiritual survival kit'. The present one requires from us, that the 'survival kit' must also contain the 'Marshall's staff' which every French soldier is supposed to be carrying in his knapsack ...

The preparation for this dual aspect of life under the beast: personal holiness and the apostolate on one side, and the active and organised resistance against the tyranny on the other, is *the same.* We have this on Divine Revelation. '*The Woman*' is with Her children in the 'wilderness', where She is in charge of preservation, sanctification and apostolate under Antichrist, represented by the

144,000 Virgins of Chapter Fourteen. And She is the *same Woman* who has been appointed by God to crush Satan's head, that is, to be in charge of the resistance, the battle and the victory, represented by the fighters of Chapter Fifteen. This stand to reason, for no one is sure if, or when, during those terrible days, one is going to be called by God to Martyrdom, or to 'survival' and personal sanctification in obscurity and anonymity, or to carry the 'marshall's baton' in fearless and active resistance. The same Woman: Our Blessed Lady and the Catholic Church, is the inspiration to all three possible outcomes. No doubt many of the 'virgins' will also be 'fighters' and vice versa. *All are moulded by the same Mother.*

To give strength to this beautiful Truth, God has left us with a witness to it. The story is so unique, it does not appear to have a parallel anywhere in the world. That makes it a 'proto-type', a 'first', from which replicas are being fashioned. It concerns a 'mother of Seven Dolours', a mother who died seven times on one day, giving up her sons one by one in martyrdom under that 'first beast': Antiochus Epiphanes, before she was finally put to death herself. That makes her a worthy prefiguration of *Our Blessed Lady*, who also gave up Her Son, the only begotten Son of the Father, to redeem the world from the tyranny of Satan; and of *our Holy Mother the Church*, who will also have to prepare for martyrdom many of Her sons and daughters, to liberate the world from the tyranny of 'the Beast'.

Since, as already mentioned, the Books of the Maccabees have such a bearing on the times under 'the beast of the Apocalypse', and since this moving story is found in these books, it will help us, if we meditate on this wonderful example provided by the Holy

Spirit, to see the Church and Our Blessed Lady at work in those days, *moulding their children in their image and likeness*, as a lesson for us in our own days of training and preparation 'in the wilderness'. For that reason it is reproduced here in full.

"There were also seven brothers who were arrested with their mother. The king tried to force them to taste pig's flesh, which the Law forbids, by torturing them with whips and scourges. One of them, acting as spokesman for the others, said,

> '*What are you trying to find out from us? We are prepared to die rather than break the laws of our ancestors.*'

The king, in a fury, ordered pans and cauldrons to be heated over a fire. As soon as they were red-hot he commanded that this spokesman of theirs should have his tongue cut out, his head scalped and his extremities cut off, while the other brothers and his mother looked on. When he had been rendered completely helpless, the king gave orders for him to be brought, still breathing, to the fire and fried alive in a pan. As the smoke from the pan drifted about, his mother and the rest encouraged one another to die nobly, with such words as these,

> '*The Lord God is watching, and surely he takes pity on us, as in the song in which Moses bore witness against the people to their face, proclaiming that "he will certainly take pity on his servants".*'

When the first had left the world in this way, they led on the second for their brutal amusement. After stripping the skin from his head, hair and all, they asked him, 'Will you eat, before your body is tortured limb by limb?' But he retorted in the language of his ancestors,

'*Never!*'

And so he too was put to the torture in his turn. With his last breath he exclaimed,

> '*Inhuman fiend, you may discharge us from this present life, but the King of the world will raise us up, since it is for his laws that we die, to live again for ever*'.

After him, they amused themselves with the third, who on being asked for his tongue promptly thrust it out and boldly held out his hands, with these honourable words,

> '*it was heaven that gave me these limbs; for the sake of his laws I disdain them; from him I hope to receive them again*'.

The king and his attendants were astounded at the young man's courage and his utter indifference to suffering.

When this one was dead they subjected the fourth to the same savage torture. When he neared his end he cried,

> *'Ours is the better choice, to meet death at men's hands, yet relying on God's promise that we shall be raised up by him; whereas for you there can be no resurrection, no new life'.*

Next they brought forward the fifth and began torturing him. But he looked at the king and said,

> *'You have power over men, mortal as you are, and can act as you please. But do not think that our race has been deserted by God. Only wait, and you shall see in your turn how his mighty power will torment you and your race.'*

After him they led out the sixth, and his dying words were these,

> *'Do not delude yourself: we are suffering like this through our own fault, having sinned against our own God; the result has been terrible, but do not think you yourself will go unpunished for attempting to make war on God'.*

But the mother was especially admirable and worthy of honourable remembrance, for she watched the death of seven sons in the course of a single day, and endured it resolutely because of her hopes in the Lord.

Indeed she encouraged each of them in the language of their ancestors; filled with noble conviction, she reinforced her womanly argument with manly courage, saying to them,

> *'I do not know how you appeared in my womb; it was not I who endowed you with breath and life, I had not the shaping of your every part. It is the creator of the world, ordaining the process of man's birth and presiding over the origin of all things, who in his mercy will most surely give you back both breath and life, seeing that you now despise your own existence for the sake of his laws.'*

Antiochus thought he was being ridiculed, suspecting insult in the tone of her voice, and as the youngest was still alive he appealed to him not with mere words but with promises on oath to make him both rich and happy if he would abandon the traditions of his ancestors; he would make him his Friend and entrust him with public office.

The young man took no notice at all, and so the king then appealed to the mother, urging her to advise the youth to save his life. After a great deal of urging on his part she agreed to try persuasion on her son.

Bending over him, she fooled the cruel tyrant with these words, uttered in the language of their ancestors,

> *'My son, have pity on me; I carried you nine months in my womb and suckled you three years, fed you and reared you to the age you are now (and cherished you). I implore you, my child, observe heaven and earth, consider all that is in them, and acknowledge that God made them out of what did not exist, and that mankind comes into being in the same way. Do not fear this executioner, but prove yourself worthy of*

your brothers, and make death welcome, so that in the day of mercy I may receive you back in your brothers' company.'

She had scarcely ended when the young man said,

'What are you all waiting for? I will not comply with the king's ordinance; I obey the ordinance of the Law given to our ancestors through Moses.

As for you, sir, who have contrived every kind of evil against the Hebrews, you will certainly not escape the hands of God.

We are suffering for our own sins; and if, to punish and discipline us, our living Lord vents his wrath upon us, he will yet be reconciled with his own servants.

But you, unholy wretch, bloodiest villain of all mankind, do not be carried away with senseless elation, crowing with false confidence as you raise your hand against his servants, for you have not yet escaped the judgement of God the almighty, the all-seeing.

Our brothers already, after enduring their brief pain, now drink of ever-flowing life, by virtue of God's covenant, while you, by God's judgement, will have to pay the just penalty for your arrogance.

I too, like my brothers, surrender my body and life for the laws of my ancestors, calling on God to show his kindness to our nation and that soon, and by trials and afflictions to bring you to confess that he alone is God, so that with my

> *brothers and myself there may be an end to the wrath of the Almighty, rightly let loose on our whole nation.'*

The king fell into a rage and treated this one more cruelly than the others, for he was himself smarting from the young man's scorn. And so the last brother met his end undefiled and with perfect trust in the Lord. The mother was the last to die, after her sons." [2 Mac. 7:1-41].

During the reign of Antichrist, Catholics too will be tempted, or even asked outright, '*to abandon the Tradition of the Catholic Church*' in favour of the 'church' that 'looks like the Lamb but speaks like the dragon'. It would then be of considerable advantage to have been *moulded by the Mother of God into the likeness of the True Church* so that we too, like 'the seven Maccabees', can have our Mother stand at our side and say to us:

> *"It was I who gave you birth into Eternal Life. In Baptism I formed you into the Image and Likeness of God your Father. I fed you with the Blessed Eucharist, strengthened you in Confirmation and instructed you in the Catholic Faith. You were married before My altar, and I entrusted to your care the children God has given you.*
>
> *Do not be deceived by this harlot 'church' which is bound to get its due punishment from God. ONLY I HAVE BEEN MADE in the image and likeness of your Blessed Mother in Heaven. She has been appointed by God to prove the stronger in this final battle for the souls of men. Honour Her by staying true to Me. Fear no one but God!*

My child, have pity on Me, so that in the Day of Mercy I may receive you back in the company of all the Saints."

'*The Marian Dimension*', so strongly prefigured by this saintly mother in the Second Book of Maccabees. This is no mere coincidence; it is God's will that we are drawn to those Sacred Pages in the Old Testament here at this point, for the conquerors of the beast in Chapter Fifteen sing in the Spirit '*the Song of Moses*', the same Song to which the 'conquerors of that first beast' referred to, under the inspiration of the same Holy Spirit. Now that God, in this way, has drawn our attention to it, may the remainder of these two Books of the Maccabees, containing the inspiring record of the Jewish Resistance against 'the first beast', be as valuable to us now in the time of preparation, as it will be to all our friends in the future.

Old Testament References in Chapter 15

There are two 'Songs of Moses', one in Ex. 15, the other in Dt. 32. 2Mc. 7:6 (quoted in Section XV) and Rev. 15:3 both refer to the second Song, Dt. 32. That way, Rev. 15:3 brings to mind Mc. 7:6. The connection? Two victories over two 'beasts' ...

Ps 92:5. [p.877]. (v.3)

'Great are your achievements, Yahweh,
immensely deep your thoughts!
Stupid men are not aware of this,
fools can never appreciate it.'

Ps 98:1. [p.881]. (v.3)

Sing Yahweh a new song
for He has performed marvels.
His own right hand, His holy arm,
gives Him the power to save.

Dt 32:4. [p.257]. (v.3)

He is the Rock, His works are perfect,
for all his ways are Equity.

Ps 145:17. [p.927]. (v.3)

Righteous in all that He does,
Yahweh acts only out of love.

Jr 10:7. [p.1270]. (v.4)

Who would not revere You, King of nations?
Yes, this is Your due.

Ps 86:9. [p.870]. (v.4)

All the pagans will come and adore You, Lord,
and will glorify Your Name.

Ex 25:22+. [p/109]. (v.5)

Inside the Ark you must place the Testimony that I shall give you. There I shall come to meet you; there, from the throne of Mercy, from between the two cherubs that are on the Ark of the Testimony, I shall give you all My commands for the sons of Israel.

1Ki 8:10-11. [p.329]. (v.8)

Now when the priests come out of the sanctuary, the Cloud filled the Temple of Yahweh, and because of the Cloud the priests could no longer perform their duties: the glory of Yahweh filled Yahweh's Temple.

Is 6:4. [p.1152]. (v.8)

The foundation of the threshold shook with the voice of the one who cried out, and the Temple was filled with smoke.

Chapter Eight

The Glorious Age of Mary

Ever since the Immaculate Conception of the Blessed Virgin Mary, the Devil has been forced to include '*the Immunity*' as a target for his attacks on 'The City of God on Earth'. In fact, the Blessed Virgin Mary and the Divinely given prerogative of Her Immunity from Original and Personal Sin, have become the focus of his attacks for two reasons:

1. God constituted THE eternal and irreconcilable enmity between 'the Woman' and Satan, and between Her Seed and his; and it is impossible to thwart Gods' Will; and
2. The Woman has become indistinguishably identified with the Bride of the Lamb of God, the one Church founded by the Son of God *in the image and likeness of His Mother*, and the instrument of His Salvation on earth.

This means that, in the war declared on the destruction of God's Redemption and Salvation, Satan was forced to make 'the Woman of Genesis' ever more, and ever more publicly, the target of his infernal attacks. Satan had wanted to avoid this at all cost. His intention was to keep the targets separate and not to involve 'the Woman of Genesis' in his war on the Church. But God had other ideas, and it is His Decree that the Two Targets are One! Helpless in the face of the Divine Will, Satan had to accept and watch with impotent rage how, as an inevitable consequence of this Decree, the discharge of Mary's divinely appointed task, *the gathering of Her seed*, became more and more pronounced and public, as the attacks on the Catholic Church became more universal, more deadly and more refined. It became impossible to hide that the Blessed Virgin Mary is a sure Haven of Refuge, a second Ark, sheltering all who come to Her in their dire afflictions.

This identification, this intimate union with the Mother of God, makes the Catholic Church unique and uniquely strong! No other 'church' has this distinction, this prerogative ... They all scotched Her 'Immunity' and any devotion to Our Blessed Lady as fast as they separated themselves from the Catholic Church. And they never recovered from it as churches, even if of late their individual members start to see, what Catholic have always known. *And the modernistic 'church of darkness' of our own time is no exception.* Its hatred for the Mother of God and Her Immunity is palpable. For it is this 'church' which is sending 'the Woman', i.e. the Catholic Church as well as Devotion to Our Lady, 'into the wilderness', into oblivion and obliteration ... That is why *IMPURITY* is overtaking this modern 'church of darkness' as fast as it is cutting itself loose from the Catholic Church, and from Our Lady's Immunity within Her as 'the pearl of great beauty'. And it will also be this Teilhardian 'church of darkness and impurity', which has already started, and will eventually lead, the persecution of all who refused to be identified with it....

Ever since that memorable day, that She was publicly seen 'standing near the Cross of Jesus', Mary has taken 'Her Second Fiat': to give birth to the Members of the Mystical Body as well as to the Head, very seriously indeed. Just as in modern day unionism, passive and lukewarm members all share in the benefits wrestled from opposing forces by the active and devoted few, so all the members of Christ's Mystical Body share abundantly in the spiritual benefits obtained for the Church by those who consciously make Mary's struggle against Satan their very own.

This dual aspect,

(i) God's revelation of 'the Marian Dimension' ahead of the growth and development of Evil on earth, and
(ii) the manifold manifestations of this Evil over the last two thousand years, has so far been the subject matter of this book.

In this we let ourselves be guided by the inspired pages of the Book of Revelation, finding ample verification in the History of the Church. The Golden Age of Marian research was ahead of, and also parallel with, the scourge of Arianism. The Rosary and Holy Scapular were ahead of the Protestant Reformation and became glorified by the Church during the 'plague of the locusts with scorpion tails'. The True Devotion was ahead of Freemasonry and became established at the beginning of the scourge of the 200 million 'horsemen with serpent's tails and heads', heralding the Great Age of the Marian Apparitions and Dogmatic Definitions, which in turn, precede the reign of the Two Beasts. And the Divine Engineer behind this whole world development, the One not only in Love with His Father's Will, but also co-substantial with It, is, as we have learnt to understand, *the Little Lamb: Christ in the Blessed Eucharist in the Sanctuary of His Church.* Over the centuries, the instruments of His Design in overcoming Evil were always first given the grace of conversion and incorporation, before obduration in iniquity kept them in a state of indefinite separation. To soften the obduration, the Motherly touch of Mary has played an important and even decisive role....

Each preparation betrays the envisaged goal or end. E.g., the architects of the modern false ecumenism outline for us the 'church' they are designing: a 'church' which they want to 'look like the Lamb but speak like the dragon'. This 'church of deception' must result from the deceitful preparations employed in its construction. This 'harlot church' will get its own reward, according to St. John.

By the same token, the 2000 year preparation employed by the Eucharistic Lamb, the intricacies of which we have followed so far in this book, must culminate in a golden era of peace, when 'the New Jerusalem' will hold its sweet dominion over all the nations, after all evil has spent its fury and force. For such results are inevitable since the clearly manifested presence of *the Marian Dimension* became incorporated as a Fifth Mark in the history of the only Church founded by Christ. *The New Jerusalem*: the final image of Our Blessed Lady as well as of the Catholic Church ... no price can be considered too high, no sacrifice too great, no preparation too long and no fight too demanding to make the Twenty First Chapter of the Book of Revelation come true.

The price paid by the victims of the 200 million horsemen and of the two beasts has been very high. But so was the price paid for us at Calvary by the Mother and the Son ... The preparation has been long and arduous. The final campaign has been taxing to the limit. But the Faith, the Hope and the Love, and all the other virtues, together with the prayers, the tears and the labour which gave Glory to God over the centuries, have shaped the New Jerusalem to come, *and are incorporated in it*! Nothing will be lost, no detail considered too small, all will be present: the Old as well as the New will have its place and its own unique relation with the Whole. The expectation of so much Supernatural Wealth, of so much happiness and peace, makes us already part of it, just as the seed embraces the plant, and the Old already lives, through anticipation, in the New ...

Mary's Faith was unique ... How God dearly loved to see it preserved on this earth in Her children, together with Her hope, Her love, Her prayer-life and Her humble obedience to His Will. And even if great human suffering had to be tolerated to bring out once again its glory in all its fullness, so be it. For the Faith of the 'Woman of Genesis', has been of tremendous value to humanity: not only to bring the 'New Adam' into existence, but also to stay faithfully at His side as the 'New Eve'. And in this She became 'the Model of the Church' and the spiritual 'Mother of all the living'. In Her image was fashioned

'the Pillar and Ground of Truth'
(*1 Tim. 3:15*; *Mater et Magistra*, 1961);
'the Standard to the Nations'.
(*Is. 11:12*; *Ad Petri Cathedram*, 1959);
'the Church of perennial youth'.
(*ibid*);
'a glorious Church without spot or wrinkle.'
(*Eph. 5:27*) :
'Our Holy Mother the Catholic Church.'

But, just as Christ was let down by His people, so the Church is very often brought into disrepute by Catholics. Yet it is always the Church who brings the straying sinners back to Her, be they a worldly Pope or Cardinal, a misleading Bishop or Priest, or simply sinful, disobedient sheep. This would be impossible if the Church Herself could go astray. Each member of the Church, from the Pope down to the most inconspicuous layman, stands in need of forgiveness and grace. Each member can receive the Sacraments to that end, but the Church cannot: *She dispenses the Sacraments.* The Church is more than all the living Catholics on earth. Even if they are all sinners, the Church Herself escapes sin. For Her Head is Divine, so is Her Life in the Holy Spirit. Our Blessed Lady is a member of the Church, and She is 'without spot or wrinkle'. 'The Church' cannot go to confession to be forgiven: the Church forgives sin in the Name of Christ. It is in Him, and in His Blessed Mother, and in the Holy Spirit, that the Church Herself is without sin, without spot or wrinkle, enjoying perennial youth, always composed of sinful members on earth, yet as a Mother always calling them back from their sinful ways. Each Catholic community, however large, is in constant need of renewal, but it is the Church who always provides this renewal. If the Church Herself could err, or sin, or go astray, who would call the erring Church back? Who would forgive Her sins, if She cannot go to confession?

Truly, then, the Catholic Church is a Mystery of our Holy Catholic Faith. We *believe* in the Holy Catholic Church. We do not understand Her. We cannot comprehend how a Body, composed on sinful members, yet is Herself without sin. (Eph. 5:27)

The Modernists delight in discrediting the Church. By pointing to Her sinful, fallible members, (especially in the past!), they want us to believe that they are revealing to us a church with a fallible, sinful *nature.* To put us 'on our guard' against Her, making us rather follow them. But such a 'caricature' is NOT the Tradition of the Church. In calling sinners back from erroneous, sinful ways, She Herself must be beyond the reach of Sin and Error, and in possession of all Truth and grace. And that is precisely so because She is firmly and irrevocably united with Her Head and with His Holy Spirit. God works the Salvation of the world through His beloved Church, and God's work and Will cannot be thwarted. But this would be the case if His chosen instrument itself could go astray and become inoperative. Individual instruments of God's grace can err and sin, and even fall by the wayside *because the Church can call them back, and renew them.* But not so the Church Herself. God would constantly have to come back on earth to rebuild and redirect His Church, for the salvation of the whole world depends on Her direction and directives.

So, if eventually the Modernists pull off the hoax of giving to the world a 'church' "which looks like the Lamb but speaks like the dragon", then this monstrosity will never be the Catholic Church no matter how many of Her influential members join up with it. For the Catholic Church simply *cannot go wrong*! She looks 'like Our Lady', and Our Lady was never deceived, nor will She ever speak 'like the dragon'.

To make us look forward to our own Church past the turmoil of sin and division, St. John provides us with a picture of a most magnificent vision in the Twenty First chapter of his Apocalypse. Even the 'Jerusalem Bible' declares that this is the Church on earth, for the pagan nations have not yet been destroyed (21:24), and still have a chance of conversion (22:2).

It is almost as if Paradise has been restored on earth, so great will be the beauty and harmony of Redeemed Humanity living together. Here, in the final pages of the Last Book of God's Holy Word, 'the Woman of Genesis' is one again uppermost in God's Mind: the Woman of the First Book of His Holy Word. And now we know the mystery of this constant thread, this Divine Perseverance. This is what 'Creation' is, and was, all about: *to provide a Mother, and a Bride, for the Son of God, the Lamb of God.* And here, at last, they are together, to display their Supernatural as well as their natural Beauty; to exert here on earth their influence for the establishment of the Kingdom of God.

What evil had to be overcome for this glorious end! Before all this became the Sacred Reality God had originally in Mind ... And how patiently has the Divine Genius of the Eucharistic King worked it all out over the centuries, in such a miraculous way that all evil would eventually be overcome, serving His own ends, yet nothing got lost that could be saved, nothing got forced that could be freely won over, nothing got allowed that would bear too heavily on weak souls. More often than not, even the instruments of His choice, on which He depended for the execution of His plans, gave way under stress and temptations. And souls He had allocated to their strength and perseverance, had to be provided for in a different way ...

What wickedness has been allowed to oppose God's Design! In Paradise. Before the Deluge. In the Old Testament. And finally in the New ... How universal has been its sweep ... How great was the suffering of Noah, and of Lot, compelled as they were to live with the evildoers of their days. And of all the Saints in the Old Covenant. Of Jesus Christ Himself ... When He saw what would be asked of His beloved followers 'to make up all that was still lacking in His own sufferings for the sake of His Body, the Church', (Col. 1:24), 'his sweat became great drops of Blood falling on the ground ...' (Lk. 22:44).

To sustain all those, His infinite Love found a way to remain always with us, at the same time that this Blessed Sacrament provided Him with the means, by which He could direct all future events according to His Father's Will '*from the Sanctuary of His Church*'. And as evil and deception, lawlessness and corruption increased once again, the form of His Church became more and more modelled on His Holy Mother, so that Her role in the designs of His Father would be carried out, until His Bride, face to face *with Satan's seed*', would be so identified with Her that the final victory went 'to the Woman and Her Seed' as one. One with Him

And now, here we are in the 'New Jerusalem', the one name that fuses so permanently the Mother and the Bride into the love for the Son and the Groom. The inhabitants are at peace, and they remember the sufferings that bought such great beatitude. In the many moments of silent prayer and contemplation before the Eucharistic Lamb, they remember in a very special way the misery of their fellow Christians during the time of the '200 million horsemen', when universal sex education and a demented 'catechetics', composed in Hell, were eating the hearts out of children and parents alike, and when it was almost impossible to believe that the sufferings under Communism, Humanism and Modernism could be surpassed by what made Daniel sick to watch: the evil under Antichrist ...

And then, and only then, will the Universal Dominion and the Divine Wisdom of the Lamb be recognised with tremendous gratitude by those in contemplation. For only then will it be fully realised what benefits their Catholic ancestors of those troublesome days did obtain in being identified with the 'Woman of Genesis': *the Woman to whom the Victory had been consigned from the Beginning.* Had they only listened to the 'church that looked like the Lamb but spoke like the Dragon', the great Bliss of the New Jerusalem would not have been theirs to enjoy. *For no other 'church' survived the ordeal* ...! No church that had abandoned belief in Her 'Immunity', love for Her Person and imitation of Her virtues. Not the 'church' in league with Teilhard de Chardin, nor any 'church' in league with the United Nations or the World Council of Churches ... Only the Church to whom Christ had given the 'Morning Star'. The One that had the Name of His Mother engraved on the columns in its Sanctuary.

And all of those who prepared the way for this Heavenly Jerusalem among men, those who overcame the beast and its false prophet, and all who gave their lives rather than accept its mark, they are living stones that make up the walls of this 'City of God'. Their love for the Mother of God, and their trust in Her, have not been in vain. It secured them an eternal place in the presence of their God, and in the 'Sanctuary of the Church' they passed on for such a glorious future to the next generation. For only in that Sanctuary are found the pillars, which have the Name of the Mother of God engraved on them.

Old Testament References to Chapter 21

Is 65:17. [p.1245]. (v.1)
for past troubles will be forgotten and hidden from My eyes.
For now I create new heavens and a new earth,
and the past will not be remembered
and will come no more to man's mind

Jb 7:12. [p.736]. (v.2)
Am I the sea, or the wild sea beast
that you should keep me under watch and guard?

Ezk 37:27. [p.1408]. (v.3)
I shall settle My Sanctuary among them forever.
I shall make My home above them;
I will be their God, they shall be My people.

Is 8:9-10. [p.1155]. (v.3)
Know this, peoples, you will be crushed.
Listen, far-off nations,
arm yourselves, yet you will be crushed.
Devise a plan, it is thwarted;
put forward an argument, there is no substance in it,
for God is with us! (Meaning of Emmanuel).

Is 25:8. [p.1180]. (v.4)
The Lord Yahweh will wipe away
the tears from every cheek;
He will take away His people's shame

everywhere on earth,
for Yahweh has said so.
That day it will be said,
'See, this is our God
in Whom we hoped for salvation ...'

Is 35:10. [p.1197]. (v.4)

They will come to Zion shouting for joy,
everlasting joy on their faces,
finished with sorrow and lament.

Is 55:1. [p.1230]. (v.6)

Oh, come to the water all you who are thirsty;
though you have no money, come.
Buy corn without money, and eat ...

2 S 7:14. [p.1410]. (v.10)

I will be a Father to him,
and he a son to Me.

Ezk 40:2. [p.1410]. (v.10)

In a divine vision He took me away to the land of Israel and put me down on a very high mountain, on the South of which there seemed to be built a city ...

Is 60:1-2. [p.1237]. (v.9f)

Arise, shine out, for your light has come.
The glory of Yahweh is rising on you,
though night still covers the earth
and darkness the peoples.
Above you Yahweh now rises,
and above you His glory appears.

Is 54:11-12. [p.1230]. (v.10f)

Unhappy creature, storm-tossed, disconsolate,
see, I will set your stones on carbuncles
and your foundations on sapphires.
I will make rubies your battlements,
your gates crystal,
and you entire wall precious stones.

Is 60:19f. [p.1239]. (v.23)

No more will the sun give you daylight
nor moonlight shine on you,
but Yahweh will be your everlasting light,
your God will be your splendour ...

Zc 14:6f. [p.1542]. (v.23)

When that day comes, there will be no more cold, no more frost. It will be a day of wonder – Yahweh knows it – with no alteration of day and night; in the evening it will be light.

Is 60:3. [p.1238].(v.24)

The nations will come to your light,
and kings to your dawning brightness.

Is 60:11. [p.1238]. (v.25f)

And your gates will lie open continually,
shut neither by day nor by night
so men can bring you the wealth of nations.

Is 35:8. [p.1197]. (v.27)

And through it will run a highway undefiled
which shall be called The Sacred Way;
the unclean may not travel by it,
no fools stray along it.

Is 52:1. [p.1227]. (v.27)

Jerusalem, Holy City,
no longer shall there enter you
either the uncircumcised or the unclean ...

Zc 13:1-2. [p.1541]. (v.27)

When that day comes, a fountain will be opened for the House of David and the citizens of Jerusalem, for sin and impurity. When that day comes – it is Yahweh Sabaoth who speaks – I am going to root out the names of the idols from the country and they shall never be mentioned again.

Jerusalem, Holy City,
no longer shall there enter you
either the uncircumcised or the unclean ...

Zc 13:1-2. [p.1541]. (v.27)

When that day comes, a fountain will be opened for the House of David and the citizens of Jerusalem, for sin and impurity. When that day comes – it is Yahweh Sabaoth who speaks – I am going to root out the names of the idols from the country and they shall never be mentioned again.

Old Testament References to Chapter 22

Ezk 47:1ff. [p.1420]. (v.1)

He brought me back to the entrance of the Temple, where a stream came out from under the Temple threshold and flowed eastwards ...

8: He said, 'This water flows east ... and into the sea. *And flowing into the sea it makes its waters wholesome* ...'

[In conjunction with Rev.22, this is a first class reference to the Eucharistic Lamb who, in the Golden Era described here, will let Grace flow into 'restless humanity' (the 'sea', remember?) and so subdue it permanently to the sweet dominion of His Church, and to the Glory of the Church, now so completely transformed through Suffering, that She displays the supernatural beauty of Our Blessed Lady in whose image She was conceived. For both, the Mother and the Daughter, are the 'New Jerusalem', the City where God loved to dwell. The same imagery is employed in the next quote to which we are referred to by the text.]

Zc 14:8f. [p.1542]. (v.1)

When that day comes, running waters will issue from Jerusalem, half of them to the eastern sea, half of them to the western sea; they will flow summer and winter. *And Yahweh will be King of the whole world.* When that day comes, Yahweh will be unique, and His Name unique ...

Ezk 47:7. [p.1420]. (v.2)

When I got back, there were many trees on each bank of the river.

Ezk 47:12. [p.1420]. (v.2)

'Along the river, on either bank, will grow every kind of fruit tree with leaves that never wither and fruit that never fail. They will bear new fruit every month, *because this water comes from the Sanctuary.* And their fruit will be good to eat and their leaves medicinal.'

Zc 14:11. [p.1542]. (v.3)

The ban will be lifted: Jerusalem will be safe to live in.

Dn 8:26. [p.1440]. (v.6)

'This explanation of the vision of the mornings and the evenings is true, but you must keep the vision secret, for there are still many days to go.'

Dn 2:28. [p.1425]. (v.6)

'... but there is a God in heaven Who reveals mysteries, and Who has shown the king what is to take place in the days to come.'

Dn 12:10. [p.1446]. (v.11)

Many will be cleansed, made white and purged; the wicked will go on doing wrong; the wicked will never understand; the learned will understand.

Is 40:10. [p.1203]. (v.12)

Here is the Lord Yahweh, coming with power,
His arm subduing all things to Himself.
The prize of His victory is with Him ...

Ps 62:12. [p.843]. (v.12)

... and You yourself repay man as his works deserve.

Is 41:4. [p.1205]. (v.13)

I, Yahweh, Who am the first
I shall be with the last.

Is 44:6. [p.1212]. (v.13)

'I am the first and the last,
there is no other god beside Me.

Epilogue

'I am the First and the Last'

It is most certainly the wish of Our Blessed Lady, that any book about Her finishes with God. 'My soul does magnify the Lord ...'

Since the 'Eucharistic Lamb' is God at the same time that He is Her Son, we may finish with Him. And now that we have seen that the Glory of the New Jerusalem is so much His patient, painstaking work over the ages, we may wish to stay there, and find some text that will combine it all for us.

Here it is:

> Zc 14:16. [p.1543].
>
> "All who survive of all the nations that have marched against Jerusalem will go up year by year to worship the King, Yahweh Sabaoth, *and to keep the Feast of Tabernacles.* (We know Who lives there!)
>
> Should one of the races of the world fail to go up to Jerusalem to worship the King, Yahweh Sabaoth, there will be no rain (Graces) for that one. Should the race of Egypt fail to go up and pay its visit, on it will fall the plague which Yahweh will inflict on each one of the nations that fail to go up *to keep the Feast of Tabernacles.* Such shall be the punishment of all the nations that fail to go up to keep the Feast of Tabernacles."

So, when that blessed time comes, there will be no excuse for not knowing to Whom all honour and gratitude of every nation on earth must go, and will go, for having achieved the Impossible. We have been told some twenty six centuries in advance ...

If in those blissful days the Church, as well as the Nations who used to war against Her, will give due honour and public glory to *the Eucharistic Lamb in the Tabernacle* for having overcome all enemies in order to take unto himself a Bride, fashioned in the glorious image of His Holy Mother, we may as well give Him all praise and cooperation NOW.

For it is right now that He is in the very process of fulfilling His Father's Will towards that blissful end, trying to fashion each one of us into a loving child of our Holy Mother the Catholic Church by giving us His Holy Mother as our Mother and Model. (Vatican II, 'Lumen Gentium').

If this little book has done something to bring you closer to 'the Little Lamb' and His Holy Designs on us all, then it was not written in vain ...

Appendix

The Power of the Blessed Virgin Mary

Whoever is interested enough to study the Development of Dogma and the history of the devotional life of the faithful, will discover that the doctrine of the Church on Our Lady grew organically from the Doctrine surrounding the Son of God made Man. Not until the big questions about Our Lord Himself and His Mission had been declared against the heretical statements of earlier times, which solutions became enshrined in the foundation dogmas of the Holy Catholic Faith, was it possible to make the other pearls in the Deposit of Faith resplendent in His Divine Light. When finally Christ's formidable Majesty stood unassailably before the world redeemed in His Precious Blood, appeared at His side, irradiated by His Light, the to us familiar figure of His Mother. For the first centuries of Christendom it became the appointed road to discover near God, next to His Son, also His Mother.

But now it is all so different. People don't care any more about the foundation dogmas of the Holy Catholic Faith. Many Catholics no longer know the difference between Protestant and Catholic Faith, so used have they become to hearing Priests talk only about 'the christian faith', as if it is all the same. As if no Martyr has ever died for the difference. For us spiritual paupers, after so much materialism, indifference and ignorance, it has become the appointed way *to discover next to Mary ... God.* This little sentence is pregnant with the whole mystery of Mary's Power. Great indeed is the glory of the Virgin, if in God, and in His Light, the Majesty of the Queen is revealed. But greater indeed is Her honour if a world heading for disaster discovers next to Mary ... God.

Conversions, the true 'miracle of Lourdes', the real 'glory of Fatima'. The Era of Mary ...

As has been made clear in this book, Mary indeed has a message for the world of today. And not only for Catholics, but for all mankind. The many who have left Christ or have forgotten Him, have entered into a world of make-belief in which they don't need Him. Whoever lost the notion of Sin no longer sees a Redeemer in Christ. Such a person will eventually accept the story 'that Christ – as God – never existed'. Human frailty is all too prone to banish from existence a God Who created Hell, and Who, as the coming Judge, has the power to punish sin severely, not only in the next life but even in this.

But Mary stands so convincingly on our side, and no make-belief is necessary to pretend otherwise, that even the greatest sinner could still within himself cherish the wistfulness of Her existence, if only as a far-away solution to problems, the sheer weight of which has become too much for him to bear. The faithful christian people know this so well, and have adorned Mary with a title which so vividly expresses Her very own power: '*Omnipotentia Supplex*' – '*Pleading Omnipotence*'. And how many are there not today, hidden in God's Church, ardently hoping and praying that the highest Ecclesiastical confirmation of this Title has been reserved for our times: the solemn declaration of another great Marian Dogma: "*Mary, Mediatrix of all Graces*". All Graces means what it says: All Graces. Even the greatest ... Whoever mediates those, is pleading omnipotent.

In our disabled world a situation has arisen where, when Christ is no longer loved and followed, Our Lady will prove to be the final ray of the most profound Mercy: the meeting place between God and His wayward creation. *A rediscovery of God* ... through the pleading powers of Mary, and to Her Glory.

If we see in this the role of the Church to the glory of the Church, it is so because – as we saw – it is the appointed role of the Woman to gather Her children. And this Woman happens to be the Mother and Model of the Church.

How is this Power of Mary revealed to us? How does it manifest itself in the ordinary existence of our everyday life? Can we really see it at work in the usual run of events?

Every catholic can tell you of favours, Divine interventions and innumerable examples of answered prayers obtained through the intercession of the Blessed Virgin Mary, the Mother of God. But, no matter how divergent all these facts may appear; ultimately they all reveal the one and the same power: Mary is capable of '*hastening God's hour*' with a human being! Awe-inspiring is the realisation of this mediation for anyone prepared to penetrate deeper into this profound Truth.

That Mary possesses the power 'to hasten God's hour with man' rests on solid evidence, facts described in the Gospel itself. I will quote here TWO instances.

I. The Wedding Feast of Cana

It is worth noting *how isolated* the First Miracle of Christ stands out against the remainder of the pattern of His Public Life. He had every reason to remain in the background for a while, and not 'offend' the hot-headed leaders of the Jews or to 'hurt' the people, living in expectation, by stating, pointing to His own poverty and humble status as a carpenter's son: '*I am your long-awaited Messiah*!' With one blow the total success of His immense Mission would have been rendered impossible. For, what the Jews were expecting with almost absolute certainty: deliverance from the Romans, He could not give them. Neither was His Mission to be identified with the restoration of their own national independence. And so it was incumbent upon Him to prepare them, with the utmost tact and prudence, for the true nature of His Commission. And that required time. A sudden confrontation with the mystical reality of the Spiritual, and from Sin redeeming Kingship of Christ – externally an ordinary Man – would have been too much to ask from the people. The contrast with what they were told to expect by their bad political leaders would have been too great. If Christ and His Messianic Mission were to be rejected in the end by the people, then this could only be done *as the outcome of a free choice*, for which full understanding, the result of careful teaching, is an integral part.

And so, in the preparation of His beloved people, extreme consideration was required of Christ.

And here He was on that wedding feast with His compassionate Mother, and Her delicate question in the extreme. For, even if His Mother did not request outright, the insinuation was all too clear and was immediately taken up by Her Son. For His plans and those of His Father She could not have chosen a more inopportune moment. Only months later, after He had acquired a certain reputation as a teaching Rabbi, 'was His Hour there' to reveal Himself also as a miracle worker *to confirm His teaching* ... Here in Cana He had nothing to confirm because He hadn't taught His people anything yet. And thus it hadn't occurred to anyone yet that He was sent from above. The totally unsuspecting guests here at Cana, flushed at that by the feast, could be forgiven if they started to see in Him what He was trying to avoid at all cost during those first precarious months, since He could never tolerate the acquisition of this image: the popular hero who would give the masses 'bread and plays'.

And now that urgent appeal from His Mother. She knew Him intimately, and never had She acted unreasonably nor ever asked Him anything She would later regret. He hesitated as if to give Her time to reconsider. He said: "My hour has not yet come ...", indicating clearly that a miracle NOW could have the most disastrous consequences, which so far he had avoided at any price.

But here we come across what could be called a 'dilemma' in Christ: "*Was the Honour of His Mother also included in that price*?" could He lower Her esteem in the eyes of a whole human history still to come? That history would contain millions upon millions of people 'of little faith', and it looks as if, just for them, this whole matter had been brought to a head by the Son, to put in the clearest possible Light the unique power of His Mother. The encouragement and reassurance He read in those wonderful eyes He would one day love to read in the eyes of all those who would model their Faith and trust on Her, a balm to His Sacred Heart amidst the coldness and indifference of the ages.

The tense drama of the moment was altogether lost on the guests, but when the six jars of wine had been unobtrusively added to the dwindling supplies, was God's Hour with human beings advanced, and had Christ given in to His Mother. With His own omnipotence and love He would carry the risk involved. In His eyes it was infinitely more important that 'we of little faith' should come to see the full revelation of the almost limitless power of His Holy Mother.

II. The Sanctification of St. John the Baptist

So too did God 'advance the hour of His Precursor' and did He receive him in Sanctifying Grace three months earlier than usual, just at the moment when, *carried in by His Mother Mary*, He met him for the first time in Elizabeth's house. If God intended to do this, He could have done it earlier. Would it have happened if Mary had not gone to visit Her cousin? We do not have to know any of this. Only one thing stands out: it did *not* happen when Mary was *not* involved; it happened when She *became* involved.

These two examples from the inspired pages of Holy Writ go to show that the hour to receive from God both spiritual and temporal favours may be advanced if the intercession of the Blessed Virgin Mary is obtained. Maybe even the whole Church could, at one stage, have been the beneficiary of this extraordinary Power, if it is true that God *hastened* to send His Holy Spirit on all the ones gathered in the Cenacle 'in continuous prayer with Mary the Mother of Jesus'. And we may piously meditate on this as a third occasion which became revealed to us through the pages of the New Testament.

Mary has penetrated most intimately into the uncreated Essence of God's Being and Knowledge. Where eventually the most ardent intelligence of the pure spirit of an Angel can advance no further, is it given to Mary to enter more profoundly into union with Almighty God, alone, all alone. Nobody can follow Her there. No one can know what, in the sacred intimacy of that union, She knows of God. No other created intelligence will ever understand what, there, in the mysterious silence between God and His Mother, it is given to Her to understand.

From Her own actions She has revealed to us that, there, in the Heart of God, She has finally come across 'the weakness of God': His Love for man ... His pure Love for the weak and the poor, and for all the ones who missed out. For the ones who are pushed away, who have come to the end of their tether, who have no more hope ... The seekers, the outcast, the lost, and the ultimate in degradation ...

And in the full possession of Her own everlasting beauty assumed into Heaven, She will recast this knowledge of the weakness of God into Her very own power, 'The Power of Mary' to hasten the Hour of God with man....

www.ingramcontent.com/pod-product-compliance
Lightning Source LLC
LaVergne TN
LVHW040216110826
845146LV00005B/1311

* 9 7 9 8 8 8 8 7 0 5 2 1 6 *